Yachtsman's Choice

Yachtsman's Choice

The Best of *Rudder*

Edited by
Gurney Williams, III

David McKay Company, Inc.
New York

Library of Congress Cataloging in Publication Data

Main entry under title:

Yachtman's choice.

   1.   Yachts and yachting—Addresses, essays,
lectures.   I.   The Rudder
VM331.Y3   1977   797.1'08   76-44337
ISBN 0-679-50661-6

10 9 8 7 6 5 4 3 2 1
MANUFACTURED IN THE UNITED STATES OF AMERICA

Foreword

Rudder has been continuously published in the United States since 1890, which gives it a life-span that covers this century and ten years of the nineteenth-century. It is the oldest boating publication we have, and it is remarkable how many generations of Americans have been nurtured by *Rudder* in its several metamorphoses (*The Rudder; Rudder, Sail and Paddle*). We at *Rudder* are constantly hearing from readers who have found collections of the magazine in the family attic—probably spanning an ancestor's boating lifetime.

What is also remarkable is how little certain elements of boating have changed since 1890. Thomas Fleming Day's broadside against New York City's scow-hauling tugs and their passages down Long Island Sound and his fulmination about the lack of knowledge of the "Rules of the Road" on the part of yachtsmen could have been written yesterday. In fact, it was apparent to me as we went through the magazine's bound volumes during the early period of research that sea stories, especially fact-filled ones are eternally interesting and useful, that stories of the love of boats and the camaraderie of cruising makes for joyful reading and vicarious sailors of us all. Contributing Editor Gurney Williams III, writer and boatman, has skillfully selected the articles, and I commend them to you.

Martin Luray
New York
November 1976

Editor's Note

You can't judge a boat by slapping the hull, listening for the quality of resonance. But you can judge a boating *story* by resonance, and that's the test I used to assemble this collection.

At its best, *Rudder* covers a lot more than boating. For instance, when Jerry Cartwright's *Scuffler* (in "Three Thousand Miles to Windward") springs a leak in the Atlantic, suddenly the story is not merely about a boat. Hard pumping saves *Scuffler*. But Cartwright's hopes are sunk, and as he ghosts back to port he has to fight to raise them. That's one kind of resonance: an overtone of human striving and passion, with boating as backdrop.

Other *Rudder* stories resound with the tone of the times in which they were written. In 1910, William Harper, Jr., taught *Rudder* readers how to pilot a biplane ("How to Fly"), and we can hear in his instructions the booming enthusiasm of that era over new and miraculous machines. By 1963, the same kind of enthusiasm had generalized into fascination with intelligence and security systems ("The America's Cup War Games"); there are chilling reverberations in the author's report on the arrest of an Australian photographer who wanted to get "an angle shot at the President."

Many of the excerpts in the first three parts of this collection reflect the first kind of resonance. They center on uncommon individuals—anxious during calms, content during gales, courtly, rough-hewn, angry, romantic. A brave woman sailing the Atlantic alone discovers that her worst enemy is her imagination ("Woman Alone at Sea"); a designer finds some cabin color schemes more nauseating than seasickness ("The Common Sense of Cabin Arrangement"). Many *Rudder* writers like these used the magazine to chart themselves—to clarify who they were and where they were going—allowing the reader to ride along in fascinating explorations.

Part 4 focuses more on the second kind of resonance, each excerpt reflecting changes in boating and the spirit of the country. Technology creeps aboard ("The Remarkable New Wave"). Fiberglass makes a successful landing ("The Fiberglass Invasion"). Technological wizards win the races ("Masters of the Jury Rig") but sometimes lose the fish ("Sailfish Showdown off Stuart").

Part 5 is a playful reprise, like the lapping of peppery little waves against a hull in a harbor after a day at sea.

The test I used in developing these sections had to be strict, because *Rudder* has grown, over 85 years, into a formidable vessel. Stacked next to each other on shelves, the 92 volumes have a length over all of more than 20 feet. They weigh more than 750 pounds. *Rudder* makes her entry in the 1890s with several fine, thin volumes. Her breadth increases in the 1920s and '30s, the volumes swollen by stories of circumnavigation and chronicles of a growing powerboat industry.

Suddenly, about 1946, the colors of the volumes change, first to light green and then in 1958 to dark blue, as if to signal some new turn in her lines, perhaps toward the age of fiberglass and the three-day weekend afloat.

There are characters at every station. *Rudder's* first editor, Thomas Fleming Day, for instance, gives bad reviews to boat builders' annual extravaganzas ("On Boat Shows"). John G. Hanna calls the America's Cup races a "very trivial subject." These men and others in this book were boatmen before they were journalists; *Rudder* let us know them at their drawing boards and at sea.

I bow to their memory, and offer thanks to all other *Rudder* contributors, past and present, whose writings have kept me company for the past six months.

I'm also grateful to Jeanne Hines, assistant editor, for helping me to prepare the manuscript, and to Martin Luray, *Rudder's* editor, for keeping today's *Rudder* salty and resonant.

—Gurney Williams ,III

CONTENTS

1

Boats and Brave Skippers

Three Thousand Miles
to Windward

by Jerry Cartwright

DECEMBER, 1972

Feeling the wind as we entered Plymouth Sound, I signaled to the skipper of my towboat. It was time to go.

There is an old Cape Horn sailing direction that reads, "Whatever you do, make westing, make westing." Plymouth Sound isn't Cape Horn, but with Newport 3,000 miles to windward, the sailing advice if you want to get there is the same. On July 17th, more than fifty boats and skippers—all entered in the 1972 Observer Single-handed Transatlantic Race—had been towed from Millbay inspection docks into Plymouth Sound, ready at the sound of a cannon shot to make westing to Newport.

3

Most were French and British. Only five of us flew the Stars and Stripes—a poor showing.

My wife had suddenly become very quiet as she waited by the lifelines, watching as I finished my preparations. Sharing the long moment together as our eyes met and locked, I knew I would never be clever enough to thank her for the constant help and support she had given me, or reassure her about the long passage ahead. We had worked long hours in bad weather—hurrying desperately to ready the boat before the deadline.

The gun was ten minutes away, and *Scuffler III*, freed from the towline and under sail, seemed to lean eagerly into the wind as we tacked toward the line. In two days of badly needed sailing trials, the little boat had exceeded all expectations—showing amazing speed for its 32 feet. LOA on all points of sailing. It was stiff and comfortable— endearing qualities on a dark, blowy night in a single-handed boat. And it balanced beautifully under its new cutter rig.

Only one nagging concern still bothered me. During the 500-mile solo qualification in heavy April weather, gale conditions had knocked the caulking out of the forward sections of the hull. The resulting leaks had nearly sunk us, and the recaulking was the one job I had not done myself. It had been a mistake, but with the time running out, I had pushed the worry out of my mind.

My watch showed 45 seconds to go, and I came over on starboard tack. Our position was good and *Scuffler* seemed to be beating to windward better than an 18-year-old warrior had a right to do. As the gun sounded, Ann Michailof, one of the women competitors, came barreling down on port tack and, violating everything but being attractive, rounded up insistently under my port side. With a soft lurch, we bumped intimately over the starting line together. The race had begun.

As the fleet beat out through the breakwater, I was elated at how well my little boat was doing at the start. We were moving past larger boats we had no business outsailing at all. The race committee had given my boat a lovely 27-day handicap, and the way it was moving now against the others, given a good passage, it seemed possible for *Scuffler* to place very close to the top. Suddenly I felt very happy to be among such a remarkable group of sailors committed to such an extraordinary task. It would have taken an unimaginative soul indeed not to have appreciated the spirit that was moving this unique collection of mariners toward Newport, 3,000 miles to the west.

By the next day, well offshore, the headwind had reached gale strength. The boat had been in far higher winds during the qualification run, but a gale from the direction you are trying to go is never pleasant. To stop the slamming, I finally hove-to under triple-reefed main and a lashed tiller.

Between the storm and watching for ships, there was very little sleep those first few days, and that small amount was done in wet oilskins. Early on the 21st, our fourth day out, with the seas still high and the wind between 25 and 30 knots, we dropped off three tremendous seas in a row, and within minutes what I most feared happened. The hull began taking water at a rate that could soon sink us.

At 0930, I entered in my log:

Evidently opened up again. Pumped 283 strokes. Seven minutes of pumping between 0815 and 0905. Certainly over 100 gallons per hour. Absolutely heartbreaking . . . Just can't conceive not finishing this race.

Forty minutes later the water was still pouring through the seams where the caulking had spewed out. And with the rising water, all hope fled for a winning passage. In fact, there seemed very little chance the hull could ever be repaired in time to even get back into the race. My morale reached some kind of record low that day, and for the first time in twenty-five years, I cried as I worked the pumps and tried to figure out some way we could continue on. Finally, I decided there was nothing to do but return to Falmouth. We ghosted in two days later on a dying breeze. I was punchy from lack of sleep, having spent most of the time manning the pumps.

Within hours after I had arrived and started looking for a good cheap yard, a huge Cornishman had four men working on my hull. Burning the paint off the forward area of the bottom, they shook their heads in displeasure over the bad caulking job—too little cotton driven in too deeply. The worst leaks were now in the garboards, which hadn't been leaking before the recaulking. As if to show how a good crew did it, they caulked her up tight again, then roughed the bare hull with a hacksaw blade and laid on two layers of nylon cloth using epoxy resin.

They were all sailors, and seemed to understand why a man would want to get back into the race so badly. They did a good job quickly, and within four days I had dropped my moorings and was once again saying good-bye to my wife.

This time she couldn't hide the fear in her eyes. For the first time in a dozen passages, she seemed to sense I had lost confidence in my vessel. I felt a great affection for the little boat because of its nonconformity and fine sailing qualities, but I no longer trusted it. But I also had had enough of second starts. I was determined nothing I found in the Atlantic would turn me east again. I feared failure far more than I feared a sinking boat.

Rounding Pendennis Point, I gave one last wave to the small solitary figure standing quietly on the quay behind me, and laid *Scuffler* off for the Atlantic beyond.

We were ten days behind the fleet now, but on the first day out, we logged 118 miles close-hauled into Force Six winds. As is often the case when you're expecting the worst, the weather turned pleasant, and I started to relax just a bit.

On the 28th, the BBC announced that Sir Francis Chichester had sent a message that he was "weak and cold" and was retiring from the race. The first report placed him 15 miles from my position. Also hearing the message, a French weather ship and a converted Danish yacht named *Lefteria*, which was flying an American flag, started a search for him. We had met a young American couple off *Lefteria* while in Falmouth for repair. So it was with keen interest I searched the horizon and listened to each news report.

On July 2nd, I heard that the weather ship had struck and sunk *Lefteria* after earlier drifting into Chichester's yacht and crippling it. It was incredibly bad seamanship, but the damage was done. Five men and two women floated dead somewhere in the Atlantic because of it.

The accident, occurring so close to my position, depressed me deeply. I felt sorry for Sir Francis. Old, fatigued, drugged on painkillers, he had made a costly mistake. But I mourned more deeply for the young couple off *Lefteria*. Land creatures, knowing nothing of the sea, they had died young and frightened in this cold, alien place.

The tragedy colored my thinking for the coming weeks. I dreaded news of any bad weather ahead. Pushed by a stupid urge to get the maximum out of the boat, I was also assailed by the belief the hull would open up again. Somehow, I connected the whole thing with my failure to complete the Single-handed Transpacific Race in '69. Battered about in heavy weather in a very light-displacement boat, I had pitched from my bunk, fracturing my skull and damaging my inner ear. Finally, half deaf, dehydrated, and too dizzy to stand without help, I had drifted into Hawaii, unable to finish my trek across the Pacific. I had always enjoyed the wild thrill of heavy weather in a small boat. Now, filled with a dread I couldn't define, I watched for every weather system with apprehension and anxiety.

That morning I hoped the feeling of vulnerability would pass. So I set about doing odd jobs on the boat—figuring that it would improve my mental outlook.

I respliced a frayed set of staysail sheets and retuned the rigging. The galley wanted a cleaning, and I dried and aired my stores. A sail needed patching. I rechecked all the safety equipment. I even practiced with my spare plastic sextant to see how closely it checked out with my number one (four miles). And I set about triangulating an engineering fault on my steering vane before it carried away.

Every day as I dropped further south toward the Azores, I entered a different page of latitude in the navigational tables. On the 10th, I changed volumes at 40 degrees, and at the same time, lost the light headwind that had carried me south so easily. For the next thirty hours I drifted through the Azores. They were so close (I slatted within three miles of Faial), and looked so inviting, that the desire to put into Horta seemed almost overpowering. I desperately felt the need to get word back to Kay. The nagging worry that all is not well on shore seems to be an affliction a single-hander must live with.

The islands were wailing a siren call into my good ear that was almost impossible to ignore. Finally, I did get a message off. Spotting a local fishing boat, I dashed off a letter, stuck it in a bottle with a dollar bill and a note in bad Spanish, and pitched it over ahead of them. The next few minutes were comical as I tried to stop them from filling the bottle with water and passing it back. At last they deciphered the note, and a week later it turned out, Kay did receive the letter.

With the letter away, I suddenly wanted to leave the islands behind. There is time when you're alone to sort out real desires and motivations. You discover that things and objects in your life have often become misproportioned; many values and directions have been wrong all along. And the really important things have been neglected and unappreciated.

At the halfway mark it looked as if we were going to make a really fast passage. With the good winds supposedly ahead, it might turn out to be possibly the fastest ever for a boat the size of *Scuffler*. But a sailor should never forget his humility. For some time I had been secretly adding the remaining days mentally, and I was happy with the figures. Then I started putting my sailing made good on the chart and stepping off the distances. The bottom fell out. One day I had made 39 miles. Another—22.

If you're a superstitious sailor you entreat the wind. You stick a knife in the boom. You whistle. You spit over the side. You urinate in the direction you want to go. Anything to get moving once again. The most important thing is to shut out the horrible sound of slatting sails and shaking spars and substitute instead that sweetest of all promises, the swift rush and bubble of the sea slipping past.

One day during the calms, two killer whales circled the boat for hours. And late one night, a large phosphorescent mass as long as the boat churned slowly in behind me and bumped against my steering vane. Another day, a very smelly sperm whale surprised me and scared me as he bashed a mighty fluke down within yards of the boat. I saw sea turtles and literally thousands of boisterous porpoises. And one evening I watched in despair as a small land bird tried valiantly to reach the stern, then dropped suddenly into the sea, exhausted and spent, to drown within a few feet of food and succor. The very mortality of the gallant, fluttering little thing transferred in my pensive mind to human mortality. I wondered how many had died in just the same way, crying tears of anguish as rescue, almost within grasp, slipped away from them.

On July 16th, I spotted an unusually large and mysterious object to starboard. Sailing slowly up to it, I logged:

> *Abeam Object X . . . Very strange creature. Seems to be some sort of stack on a boiler. But . . . why so buoyant and bobbing. Maybe it's a piece of space junk . . .*

About 12 feet tall and 5 feet across at the base, it looked suspiciously like the business end of a rocket. Whatever it was, it didn't appear to be at all happy out there. It seemed to be bobbing about in a most indignant manner, as if knowing it shouldn't be there at all, but trying desperately not to look awkward and out of place. I watched it grow smaller and smaller against the horizon as the wind freshened.

All during the long stretch of flat weather, I had noticed considerable amounts of rubbish—mostly foam and plastic—floating on the surface. Visible only during flat calms, the quantity if not the quality, seems to me to increase with every passage I make. As an experiment, during one four-hour trick on the tiller, I counted twenty-eight separate bits of rubbish. My rather crude observation covered an area of about two square miles; projected over the whole ocean, that's a lot of garbage in the water.

As we neared the Gulf Stream, the weather deteriorated. There were still calms, but they were interspersed between a series of small depressions that began sweeping in from the west. A flicker of breeze would start from the southwest, and within a few hours it would be blowing westerly 25 to 40 knots before veering to the northwest and finally dying hours later, leaving a big slop.

From the beginning, the wind had been constantly on the nose, but this new set of conditions was the most frustrating I had ever experienced. Ordinarily, I would have run off to Bermuda, but Newport lay to the northwest now, and it seemed as if we would never make it on this windward course. And with heavy weather, the old dread of opening up returned. I spent chilled, agonizing hours in the cockpit as I forced us to weather, unable to endure the racket and clatter below as we slammed into the heavy seas.

I had stores and a six-man emergency life raft on deck ready to inflate, and I felt I could stay at sea for months, if necessary. But I also felt that *Scuffler III* and I deserved to be able to sail to our limits on this trip even though it was too late to come in among the leaders. I had come a long way and spent considerable effort (and practically all of our money) to make the passage. So I kept us driving in the squally conditions, never striking a sail day or night until conditions called for it, and constantly heading up, trying to make our westing.

On the 24th, during a gale, I awoke abruptly to a screaming squall that threatened to jerk the mast and rigging down around my head. Under storm sail, we had been forcing to weather as yet another small depression moved in. Exhausted from the effort of changing sails and the mental fatigue brought on by constant worry about the hull, I had finally collapsed in my oilskins below. By the time I reached the deck, befuddled and dizzy from the short sleep, we were laid rail down with a violent wind busily at work wrecking my mainsail. Three batten pockets were tcrn out before I could heave it down and get it safely below. Reporting into my log I noted:

*All hell broke loose. Caught a squall with over 50 knot winds
in it. Repairing main.*

There were seven dismastings in the race. One of them happened to
a friend the same night only 60 miles north of my position. Still 1,000
miles from Newport, I had caught up with Australian Murray Sayle
aboard his 41-foot catamaran just in time to share the same nasty little
gale. The squall had been just strong enough to blow Murray's mast into
the sea.

An American Coast Guard vessel which happened to be passing
through the area had intercepted his call and located his position within
hours. "We'll give you a tow," they had shouted. "But you'll have to
go where we're going."

"Where's that?" Murray had asked.

"Newport," the Coast Guard had answered, and thrown him a
line.

I didn't see Murray as he swept by in style, but he saw me. In 1969,
when I was qualifying for the Pacific race, I had bought a xenon buoy
marker to hang from my backstay. I've carried it around with me since.
Often controversial, its legality a bit cloudy, the blinking light can still
be seen miles farther at sea than any set of navigational lights yet devised
for a small boat. The cutter picked up my xenon light a few miles to the
north.

Scuffler and I were in the Gulf Stream now, and on August 1st, I
awoke to find a rail down and the wind wailing all too familiarly in the
rigging.

At 1300 hours I logged:

*Seas chaotic—two wave patterns. Overcanvassed. Pound-
ing . . . One gets the impression that things just continue
until something breaks.*

An hour later I noted:

*Just can't believe this series of systems is normal. Wind seems
to be right out of the west. . . . The futility of it all. Why don't
I just heave-to? It kills me not to be moving but must spare
boat.*

At 1600:

Too much canvas . . . now blowing 45 knots . . . I'm hungry, tired, wet, cold, and nervous that a ship is going to drill us, and wishing this infernal wind would cease . . . Will we ever reach Newport?

This was the fifth time the winds had held consistently above 40 knots since the start, but somehow in my mind, this gale seemed to represent them all. We had weathered the others, but caught in this Gulf Stream current that had always made me feel uneasy and nervous, I once again took up my old position in the cockpit, and watched the seas as they built and grew.

As the wind veered abruptly to the northeast, the increasing force of the wind striking more directly into the current seemed to be causing the steep seas to literally explode. With a jolt, I realized I had tried to hold our course too long. We were still carrying sail, and half hypnotized by the wild scene around me, I had put us into grave danger.

Snapping on my harness line as I prepared to race forward and drop the tiny storm sails, the sea seemed suddenly to vomit aboard, and I was thrown through the lifelines and jerked against the hull as I hit the end of my slender line. Long ago I had promised myself I would never leave the cockpit in heavy weather without being attached. That promise probably saved my life. Hauling myself aboard, I frantically crawled forward to drop the sails and slow us down. Two more seas boarded before I could claw down the flogging scraps of sail and run us off before the raging chaos that seemed intent on burying us. I traded the urge to make westing for a considerably stronger urge to stay afloat and streamed warps from the quarters to slow us down even more.

The gale would rage around us for several hours yet, but running downhill we were reasonably safe, and I set about repairing the damage. I had bashed a kidney when I went over the side, and had a nosebleed. *Scuffler*'s cockpit dodgers were in tatters, several stanchions were bent and sprung, and the steering vane needed immediate attention, but we had both escaped with minor damage. And we weren't leaking. The little boat had finally taken all the North Atlantic had offered, and had been a staunch companion when the going was rough. I needn't have worried.

Now the dread and anxiety that had been such unwelcome ship-mates on this voyage seemed suddenly to vanish. At last I knew we were going to make it. And as my confidence flooded back, Newport seemed so close and accessible that I felt I should be able to see it although it was still 300 miles to the west.

On August 4th, we logged 144 miles and at 0900 on the 5th, we crossed the finish line at Newport—39 days, 2 hours, and 3,527 logged miles out of Plymouth. With ten days added on for the first attempt, we placed twenty-fifth on handicap. Without them, we would have been fourth. But the standings seemed unimportant—any finisher in this event had already won his own race in his own way.

Scuffler was undercanvassed now in the lee as we worked slowly toward the inner harbor. But the race was over, and what sails we carried didn't seem very important. Suddenly we appeared to be tacking through half of the big shiny yachts on the Eastern seaboard. It was the New York Yacht Club's annual cruise outward-bound making a spectacular sight to someone who hadn't seen another sailboat for over a month.

As I threaded through the imposing fleet, three or four crews gave me a wave. Perhaps I was being overly sensitive as I sailed abruptly into the civilized pack, but I received a definite impression that my funny looking little cutter bearing its Atlantic scars—steered by a rather frayed skipper in tattered oilskins—didn't quite meet approval. We seemed to be staring at each other from different worlds.

Nearing Port of Call Marina, I spotted fellow competitor Jock McLeod, skipper of *Ron Glas*, waiting to take my lines. As I stepped ashore, Jock handed me a beer and shook my hand.

"Well done, mate," he said. The race was over.

Aboard with
Captain Barr

by L. Francis Herreshoff

MAY, 1948

America's Cup challengers and defenders around the turn of the century were Brobdingnagian boats with delicate spars and sky-filling sails. Designer L. Francis Herreshoff called the 90-foot 1903 defender Reliance, *for instance, an "extreme racing freak," with "lighter spars and rigging per square foot of sail area than any yacht built before or since." It was a feat in itself, Herreshoff said, to nurse a boat like* Reliance *through a season of racing with intact spars.*

Captain Charley Barr brought Reliance *home without mishap that season, and saved the cup. He had defended against other challenges in*

1899 and 1901 as skipper of Columbia, *a record that bolstered his reputation as the greatest racing skipper of his era.*

Perhaps his secret was that he was a gentleman. "His manner with his officers and crew was quiet and dignified," said an English magazine after his death in 1910. "And the extraordinary amount of shouting that goes on aboard many English vessels was absent on the yachts under his command."

Here's a portrait of Captain Barr at the helm.

Captain Barr was in some ways unique among yacht captains. He seemed perfectly content to stay aboard ship all the time excepting for the morning marketing and getting the latest newspaper. He was always neatly dressed and seemed to get up that way very early in the morning. He planned a complete day's work for each of the crew, and although all hands were busy all of the time, the yacht was always ready to receive the owner or guests and could have been gotten under way at a moment's notice. Which is in great contrast to most yacht captains of that time, who only dressed up to go ashore to spend the evening in some gin mill, or to boast on some pierhead till the small hours of the morning.

Captain Barr's crews seemed quick, willing, and contented. Their principal ambition seemed to be to please their captain, so that everything went off like clockwork and the meals were good and on time. Yes, Captain Barr loved to be aboard ship, but best of all he liked being under way and sailing. And when everything was straightened out and he sat at the helm with his eye on the luff of the topsail, he was the picture of contentment. I must say I never saw an owner who began to get the pleasure out of sailing or racing that Captain Barr did. He seemed never to be under tension in a race, and could steer the yacht by instinct while carrying on a conversation or perhaps telling some funny incident of past yachting.

When so inclined, he could be most entertaining and agreeable to the owner and guests, which certainly is not so of most skippers, particularly the amateurs who seem to take racing so seriously that they cannot bear to have anyone speak when they are steering. However, Captain Barr did not speak to any of the crew when under way except when giving an order. When he was on one of the larger yachts, he was a strict disciplinarian. He had trained his first mate (who for several years was Chris Christiansen) to keep one eye on him, and when Captain Barr wished to give an order he simply crooked his forefinger slightly, whereupon the mate came close to him. Then Captain Barr would say very quietly but distinctly: "Mr. Christiansen, after rounding the next mark I would like the spinnaker set to starboard. I would like the jib topsail replaced with the ballooner."

The mate would then pace slowly up and down the deck, watching the marker they were approaching until he estimated the right time and distance to commence action. Then he would roar out, "Take in the yib topsail. Raus mit the spinnaker pole to starboard. Stand by for a yibe." Before this moment everything was quiet, the crew of some twenty men all lying prone in a neat row with their heads near the weather water-ways. The second mate crouched in the leeward fore rigging watching the headsails, and the only sound to be heard was the swish and hiss of the waves under the leeward bow, and a low moan of the wind in the rigging. But now the yacht's deck suddenly changed to a scene of intense activity as each man scrambled to his station and stood crouched, ready for action, some at the sheets, others at the upper and lower backstays, while the spinnaker pole was being run out and the men on the bowsprit had muzzled the jib topsail.

Now the mate nods his head at the mastheadsman, and this agile fellow runs up the mast hoops like a monkey climbing a ladder and stands on the fore spreaders in anticipation of changing the main topmast staysail. Now the mark buoy is almost abeam, and the yacht swings like a gigantic turntable as Captain Barr crouches to leeward of the wheel and pulls the spokes toward him, hand over hand. The yacht now rights herself, and the wind, which had seemed quite strong, suddenly becomes very light as the yacht, which before was heading into it at some 7 or 8 miles an hour, now goes with it, making the difference of some 14 miles an hour to the wind's apparent velocity. But in the meantime there is the clicking of many winches and the chorus of many orders as the second mate and the two quartermasters call out in broken English strange words that are instantly understood and obeyed. Some of the orders are, "Stand by the after spinnaker guy," and "Overhaul the leeward backstays," and the whole yacht seems to quiver from the stumping forward and aft of several 200-pound Swedes, when crisp and clear the first mate calls out, "Yesus, don't younce de yacht."

The spinnaker and balloon jib are now broken out almost simul-taneously, and the balloon main topmast staysail is going aloft. Soon everything quiets down again and the only movement is a few hands coiling down sheets and halliards. Captain Barr has now moved back of the wheel and stands with his eye on the telltale pennant at the peak of the club topsail. He seems perfectly cool and quiet, and no one would have guessed his eye had seen anything but the mark buoy, the compass, and the luff of the topsail. And, furthermore, anyone would have thought the maneuver had been perfectly performed, would have thought the crew had performed miracles of sail-changing in almost seconds. But now Captain Barr crooks his forefinger again and the mate approaches him, saying, "Yes, sir," and Captain Barr says, "Mr. Christiansen, that was done very well, but the next time I would like to see the club sheet slacked simultaneously with the foresheet." "Aye, aye, sir," says the mate as he moves to the weather main rigging with one eye on the luff of the spinnaker.

Now the men are all sitting up on deck, ranging aft from the forecastle hatch to the weather backstays, when silently the jib topsail is handed up, stretched aft, and the men kneel in a straight row, each bending over and pulling a piece of stopping thread from the mop-like hank attached to his waist a little aft of starboard. Each man rolls the sail up to its luff rope, ties a few stops, and almost before you know it the jib topsail again disappears forward.

Now eight bells is struck, and there is a slight movement at the fore hatch. The second steward is passing up great thick sandwiches and a bottle of beer for each man. If the jib topsail had been stopped up rapidly, the sandwiches and beer were now being stowed away even more rapidly. Many of Captain Barr's crew were large, handsome fair-haired sailors of middle age with Viking-like moustaches, and many of them had sailed under him for several years and were perfectly trained. After being trained, these Nordic crews that Captain Barr specialized in were very quick workers. Each man was a machine that could understand and execute orders without stopping to think what he was doing, so that the yacht had one head or brain (the captain), several mouthpieces (the mates), and twenty or so bunches of sinew, muscle and leather which acted instantly at each order.

The yacht is now rolling slowly back and forth as the spinnaker pole rises and settles, and the great billowing spinnaker and balloon sails pull alternately on one side and the other. The contrasts and shades of colors through the sails are always changing so that the yacht seems a great iridescent being of opalescent color—the heavy mainsail of grayish white, the club topsail of creamy yellow, the spinnaker and balloon jib of transparent pinkish tan, and now and then a shadow from a spar or sail reflecting the blue of the sky and sea in a light violet shade. The Oregon pin spars of rich amber and gold, the teak rail cap, the snowwhite decks and uniforms of the crew, the polished bronze, all seem alive and moving as they sparkle in the reflection of the sun.

This is but a glimpse of yachting at the turn of the century in the time of Charley Barr, when yachting was at its zenith, but, alas, now all gone and only a memory like the square-rigger, for the large steel schooner is gone, the crews which manned them are gone, and the captains who could manage them are gone.

Kidnapped

by William Albert Robinson

APRIL, 1932

Robinson and his 35-foot ketch Svaap *covered close to 30,000 miles in a world-circling cruise from June, 1928 to November, 1931. Few parts of his story—carried by* Rudder *for several years beginning in 1929—are as hair-raising as this account of his seizure by Arabs while "reef crawling" up the Red Sea with his Tahitian mate Etera.*

We progressed slowly for several days after leaving the island of Kamaran, groping along through an annoying sand haze from the desert, unable to see reefs or little sandy islets until almost upon them. Nights we anchored in uncharted lagoons or behind offshore reefs, avoiding the few settlements we saw because of the fearsome reputation of the inhabitants. The scorching arid breath of the desert alternated with the saturatingly humid sea wind. Both felt as if they came straight from the door of a blast furnace. Even at night the temperature was 95° or more. Strangely enough, Etera, child of the tropics, felt it worse than I did and was constantly complaining. It was a parched and sunburnt land of endless forlorn sand dunes.

Then one day the barometer tumbled, and from the south came a driving gale. In company with a large cumbersome Arab dhow we flew down the coast seeking shelter. I planned to find a little anchorage called Khor Nohud on the chart. Just before we reached it, the dhow turned in through a different break in the shore reef. Confident that they, with local knowledge, had chosen the best shelter from the storm, I cautiously followed them into a snug little corral-girt basin.

An hour later we were prisoners, not of the swarthy Arabs that manned the dhow, but of the white-robed Emir [an Arabian chieftain] of El Birk—the fantastic Bedouin village of conical brush huts and stone houses that hung beneath a few palms on the barren burnt hillside.

I had seen it coming, when a boatload of heavily armed men put out from shore, but we were trapped. Even if we'd had time to escape it was impossible, for the dhow had shifted to a position that blocked the narrow pass. Resistance was out of the question. It was a hundred to one.

They clambered aboard and indicated by signs that the Emir wished to see me. Taking some of the ship's papers along, I went, not knowing whether I was attending a reception or my funeral. I never saw the papers again.

We climbed to the village and through its disorderly alleys to the Emir's fortified palace, where we entered through an embrasure in the wall. Across the courtyard we went, silently. It was filled with strange, staring Bedouins. Then up a dark stair onto a walled terrace, where the others left their sandals. We entered a small square room with heavily barred windows, and benches covered with Persian rugs around all four sides. There was no other furniture except a bare table with two books and a silver-handled lash.

Facing us from a niche at the opposite side, sat the Emir—enormous in his voluminous robes. Surrounding him, all around the walls, sat twenty-four lesser chiefs in picturesque garb. I was presented and seated in a dripping silence. Two riflemen guarded each side of the door.

Through a useless interpreter who knew less than a dozen words of French, I essayed a speech full of blithe lies as to my pleasure at being there. After an extended exchange of compliments, I was given to understand that I was being held for ransom. I wrote and signed a letter stating my situation, and they sent it off somewhere by camel courier. I never did learn its destination.

If I am ever kidnapped again I hope I fall into equally hospitable hands. Complaining of the discomfort ashore, I was finally allowed to live aboard the *Svaap* under guard. When I sent word that our prolonged stay meant a food shortage, the Emir at once sent a whole flock of chickens aboard, and the *Svaap* looked like a floating henhouse. I was a model prisoner, behaving as if I enjoyed it all in order to put them off their guard. When the sentries found it tedious and confining aboard the *Svaap*, it was not too difficult to bribe them to watch us from the nearby dhow.

I was full of plans of escape but could do nothing with the dhow in her present position, blocking the only exit. We had two trumps, which the Arabs had overlooked in not searching the *Svaap*. In a locker under my berth lay several guns and plenty of ammunition. Hidden in the gloom beneath the bridge deck was a shapeless object covered with a tarpaulin—the unsuspected engine. Had they so much as dreamed we had power, things would have been different.

Our chance came with the termination of the southerly blow. The wind changed to northwest and necessitated the shifting of anchors since there was not room enough for the boats to swing in the confined little basin. We helped the dhow move hers first, seeing to it that they were placed so as not to interfere with our preconceived plan. Then, ostensibly to keep the *Svaap* from going on the rocks while moving her heavy anchor and chain, we placed a light kedge on a manila line near the pass—just where it would be best for a quick exit. Dropping astern on this line, we hove up on our heavy anchor until it swung clear of the water.

The Arabs on the dhow, not more than fifteen yards away, watched with interest the proceedings whereby two men could execute a maneuver that required half a dozen in their case. From the corner of my eye I studied their faces. No sign of suspicion showed.

"Now is the time!" I whispered to Etera.

Without haste, as if we were merely moving up to place our big anchor, we hove on the manila line. Slowly the *Svaap* swung, until she was heading straight out of the pass. When we were nearly over our light anchor I went below and slipped the guns on deck behind the cabin house.

Then things started to happen. The engine, already primed and coaxed, started with a roar—full speed ahead. I flew on deck, grabbed a gun in each hand, and put a shot or two over the decks of the dhow. Every Arab dropped out of sight behind the bulwarks of the craft amid a confusion of incoherent shouting. Etera got in the small hook as we slid over it, gathering momentum as we went. A second later we were gliding between the narrow jaws of coral that formed the pass. Covering the dhow all the while, we steered for open water, keeping that bulky craft between us and the village as a shield from shore guns.

There was a great hullabaloo on shore and a random shot or two as Arab sheiks in flowing robes rushed about among the crowd on the rocky slopes. The northwest wind prevented the sailing craft from negotiating the pass, so pursuit was impossible. We would not have feared it, anyway, for our high-power rifles would have kept them at a distance.

We were free, but our problems were by no means solved. Our protecting string of offshore reefs had become a prison, confining us to a narrow shoal-infested strip of water close to this piratical coast. More than a hundred miles of this intricate channel remained, and even then, before we could escape to sea we had to get some supplies somewhere. We did have our flock of chickens. I felt that it was adding insult to injury to not only escape from my friend the Emir, but to carry off a dozen of his best chickens besides. Had there been time, I should have returned them to him beforehand.

The only place that offered any chance of getting supplies before we got to Jidda was Lith, a hundred miles north. The pilot book was a bit discouraging about Lith, saying of the inhabitants: ''In ordinary times piracy and robbing the few pilgrims who attempt to pass through to Mecca are added to their usual means of gaining a livelihood.'' It neglects to specify what the ''usual means'' are, although I strongly suspect it is something nefarious. Pilots and charts are usually unduly discouraging. Half the islands in the South Pacific are called ''hostile,'' whereas their people are the friendliest imaginable. Therefore, I did not take the warning too seriously. Besides, piracy or no piracy, we had to get food.

One evening, after three days of nerve-wracking navigation, we found our way through a winding passage into the inner anchorage of Lith. It was a great disappointment—merely a small settlement of squalid mud houses, instead of the populous town we had expected. As at Khor El Birk, the shore at once disgorged upon us a boatload of truculent Arabs who tried to inveigle me ashore. This time I was not so easily caught, and they finally left. We were tired, and soon turned in for the night, sleeping on deck.

Our ship's clock was just striking the eight bells of midnight. I awoke with a start and thought for a moment I was having a nightmare, for I looked into the muzzles of a motley assortment of firearms. A smoking oil lamp was held on high by a bulky, black-bearded giant with one eye. The flickering light fell on the wildest-looking gang of pirates I ever hope to see. There were more than a dozen of them, and more waiting in the boat which lay alongside. Every man of them was a walking arsenal, bearing rifle, revolver, and one or two knives or a sword.

There was no temporizing with this crowd. I tried to joke it off but instantly realized that these were not the polite captors of El Birk. They simply poked a gun in my ribs and took me along without even letting me dress. I did slip on a bathrobe, but that was all.

Two stayed to guard Etera, who was speechless with fright. As we rowed off, I shouted what I fully believed to be my last instructions to him—to try to escape on some passing dhow and tell the story to the first Europeans he met. Somehow, I felt very melodramatic at that moment. I was certain that I would never see *Svaap* again, and I kept my eyes on her until she faded into the black of night.

Three horses were waiting on shore, beautiful Arabian steeds, without saddles. I have always dreamed of riding a real Arabian under the stars of Asia, but never in my wildest fancies did I imagine such a ride as I had that night as we galloped bareback over the rolling desert sands. In front of me rode the chief, his white mantle fluttering from his head like the wings of a phantom. Immediately behind me rode the guard, brandishing his old French musket toward the middle of my back. I expected a shot at any moment, and curiously enough was quite calm about it, wondering what it would feel like when it came. I believed I was being taken out into the desert to be killed where there would be no trace. Then they would go back and scuttle *Svaap*. I learned that night what a condemned man feels like when he is being led out to the gallows.

My predominant thought was that no one would ever know what had happened. This worried me. People would say, ''I told you so; the boat was too small. It was a foolhardy thing to try to sail around the world in that thing.'' I did very much want to complete the trip successfully, to demonstrate that it was not foolhardy, that a well-designed, well-built small boat could go anywhere safely if properly handled.

On and on we galloped, over the rolling desert dunes. The hot wind was oppressive. The stars shone overhead. My long bathrobe flapped ridiculously in the wind, and I began to have painful reminders that I was unaccustomed to this form of violent exercise, not to mention the fact that I had never before ridden bareback and stirrupless. I longed to reach our destination, whatever it was.

After a while, we came to a lone, grotesquely dwarfed tree, where we stopped. The guard gave a peculiar cry, which was answered from somewhere in the dark. My heart beat rapidly, for I thought that this was to be the spot. But then a man appeared, examined us, and we moved on again. Then we came to an oasis with a considerable settlement. There, grimly commanding its surroundings from a rise, stood a low, square, turreted fortress with round towers at the four corners.

A few minutes later I took stock of my situation from a suffocating low cell in the fortress. There was no window or opening in the wall of any sort except the heavily barred door through which I had entered. There was not a single object in the room. The only break in the monotony of the four walls was a niche cut in the stone of one side, deep and long enough to form a sleeping shelf. A few rays of light from a lamp hung outside filtered through a small aperture in the door. There was no possibility of escape.

In this hopeless condition I languished for what seemed like a week, unable to distinguish day from night. Occasionally some peculiar tough bread-like stuff was passed in with foul water. Eventually some important Emir or Shiek arrived and examined me. We talked for hours, but as there was no interpreter I do not know what it was all about. As a matter of fact, I have never, to this day, understood the whole affair. There was no effort to take *Svaap*. I was never even searched. No effort was made to get ransom. I believe they got cold feet for some reason or other.

I was almost disappointed eventually, that it all ended as tamely as it did.

I was allowed to go back to *Svaap* under guard to get some very important diplomatic papers I claimed in sign talk to have. With the aid of some old bills of health, plenty of red ribbon, and sealing wax, I hurriedly manufactured some of the most awe-inspiring documents ever seen. I had no seal with which to stamp the sealing wax, but used the ornately figured cut-glass stopper from a Coty's Eau de Cologne bottle. This made a very impressive seal. These formidable documents so impressed the Emir (who had not the slightest notion what they were all about) that I was not returned to my cell but was to be detained in port indefinitely, why I don't know.

I soon found that the chief of the guard hated the Emir. Judicious bribery made him my ally, and we were able to get supplies aboard. A large Arab dhow lay alongside with a cutthroat crew of part-time pirates and slave-runners. The captain, an enormous jovial Arab, squeezed himself into all possible corners of the *Svaap*, exclaiming like a child over a new toy at all the curious things he saw. I gave him some charts which delighted him beyond measure. We became great friends, my pirate captain and I.

So everything was prepared for escape number two—probably the best-directed, most thoroughly sure escape ever known. The chief of the guard, in order to repay the Emir for some past injury, agreed not to guard us, although we could not leave openly by daylight, for there were some members of the garrison who were faithful to the Emir. This was where the dhow captain came in. He knew the reefs like the palm of his hand, and it was his job to lead us out in the night.

That last night will always linger in my memory. It was the only time I saw the Arabs throw off all restraint. We were aboard the great clumsy dhow—we three conspirators and the entire crew of the dhow—a wild, fearsome crowd. Drums were produced, and all night long we sang and danced to strange tempos, drinking a peculiar aromatic liquor. Different members of the crew burlesqued as women and performed weird evolutions. Even the gigantic captain did his bit, casting off all but a loincloth and violating his corpulent body with a sword dance something like one I had seen at Makalla. I even felt ashamed that I had my gun in my pocket. It was an unnecessary caution, for these good-natured pirates had accepted me as one of them.

The east was beginning to streak a little with a warning of approaching dawn when the great sail of the dhow creaked its way aloft and I bade farewell to my new-found friends. They got under way before a gentle desert breeze, and we followed close upon their heels in *Svaap*, twisting and turning in a serpentine path through unseen reefs. Dawn was breaking when we left the outer reefs behind. We headed north, and the dhow turned south.

A last farewell came floating across the purple water from that gigantic Arab sailor whose heart was solid gold.

"Salaam, America, Salaam!"

Across the Pacific
in an 18-Footer

by Captain Frank Jansen

APRIL, 1933

Fred Rebell had practically no money and no experience at sea when he struck out from Australia on his dangerous voyage. Rebell was a native of Latvia, and a builder and contractor in Australia for years before the trip; there's no explanation of why he wanted to leave.

An editor's note atop this account suggested that other people with similar plans should stay home. "We do not recommend that anyone venture to follow his example," it said.

Lack of sufficient money or experience in small-boat sailing on ocean voyages did not deter Fred Rebell from sailing single-handed in an

18-foot sloop across the Pacific from Australia to Los Angeles, California.

His total funds for boat and equipment amounted to exactly $250. He left Sydney, New South Wales, on December 31, 1931, in the sloop *Elaine*. The vessel was an old Port Jackson racing sloop with a center-board and long bowsprit, about as unfit a craft as one could choose for such an undertaking. Her measurements were 18 feet overall with 7 feet beam and 18 inches draft. Her freeboard amounted to only 20 inches. She had an open cockpit, which Fred Rebell covered over with a piece of canvas; he painted the forward part black to make it watertight and rigid, while the after half was arranged to fold back in fine weather or cover the cockpit fully when it was blowing. This improvised cabin held all his belongings, including food, water, and nautical instruments needed for such a voyage. Rebell's bunk was made out of a piece of canvas stretched over a wood frame which he could slide forward when not in use. He had a seat on each side of the cockpit measuring about 16 inches. This is where he had to do all his cooking, navigating, and reading. He prepared his meals on a small Primus stove, which he set in a cut-down gasoline can. Food and water were stowed in old 5-gallon gasoline cans with screw caps. To protect the tins against corrosion, he painted them black. Forty gallons of water were carried in this manner. One gallon of water lasted him three days, so he had ample for his needs. For food he carried flour, yeast, unpolished rice, rolled oats, pearl barley, peas, beans, wheat, cocoa, sugar, and powdered milk; at times he caught a fish. He did not have any kind of meat, nor did he carry food in tins, as this would have been too expensive. The total amount spent for food and nautical equipment was only $125.

All of Rebell's navigational instruments, excepting a watch, were homemade. He manufactured his sextant out of a piece of hacksaw blade and two pieces of iron forming a triangle. The hacksaw teeth were used in the same manner as the teeth of a modern micrometer sextant. Into these teeth he fitted a wood screw with a large brass head. This wood screw worked alongside the hacksaw teeth like the tangent screw travels along the arc of a micrometer sextant. The degrees on the arc of the instrument were painted in white paint. The large brass head of the screw had graduations of sixty minutes on it, similar to a micrometer, and every full turn of the screw advanced the index arm one degree on the arc. The index and horizon glasses were made of a highly polished stainless-steel knife blade. For an eye piece he had attached a boy scout telescope. This is the most unusual sextant I have ever seen. I compared this homemade instrument with a modern micometer sextant and came to the conclusion that one could find one's position within about thirty nautical miles correctly, although Fred Rebell tells me that he found his position within two miles of the actual latitude and longitude. But then one part of the ocean looks exactly like another, so it really does not matter who is correct.

He navigated mostly by latitude, taking sights with intervals up to nine days between observations. Rebell did not employ dead reckoning, but having found his latitude at noon, would be able to work an afternoon longitude sight without much trouble or great inaccuracy. The method of correlating his observations in the form of the "Day's Work" was not known to him. He had bad luck with his timepiece, as the humidity changed its rate considerably after he had left Sydney. At times he lost track of the date. To again find the correct day of the year he would look at the moon and compare it with the phase given in the Nautical Almanac, then take an observation of the moon and sun, both for longitude at about the same time. Then he computed the moon observation with the date he judged it to be from the size of that heavenly body and also worked the sun sight with the same date. If both longitudes fell closely together, he would know that he had guessed the correct day of the year; if not, he would try to work the sights with different dates till they gave approximately the same position. When this happened, he again knew what day of the month it was.

To save money, Rebell spent considerable time in the public library in Sydney and made copies of the charts he needed. The navigation necessary for such a voyage he also acquired from books in the public library, supplementing the knowledge gained there by purchasing a book on navigation written in 1863. In Pago-Pago, American Samoa, he received a present of some charts.

He arrived in Suva, Fiji Islands, on March 2, 1932, having taken sixty-one days for this traverse. From here he sailed to Naitauba, Apia, Danger Island, Christmas Island and Honolulu. To reach Los Angeles from Honolulu he took sixty-six days.

On January 8, 1933, he arrived in Los Angeles Harbor having been on the way one year and eight days. Good luck had practically followed him all this time, until on January 11th it suddenly changed. In the early hours of that day one of the fiercest "Santa Ana" gales coming out of the Great American Desert that ever struck Southern California broke over San Pedro Harbor, tore the *Elaine* with Rebell on board from her moorings, and threw her up on Cabrillo Beach, straining her frames, breaking her bowsprit, and causing such damage that she will not be able to go to sea again. So came to an untimely end the voyage of *Elaine*, the smallest craft that ever sailed from Australia to the North American continent.

But Fred's troubles had just begun. Having lost his boat, he was compelled to live on shore, and as he had failed to supply himself with the necessary papers when leaving Sydney, the American immigration authorities stepped in and arrested Rebell, locking him up in the local immigration station, for they considered him an undesirable alien. Not till he is able to raise $500 cash bond will he be permitted to go free in the States. This seems very unlikely, and the American immigration authorities will no doubt deport him to the country of his birth.

While many persons on shore do business on a shoestring, Fred Rebell did his voyaging on a spunyarn—and a mighty frayed one at that. The boat and sail cost him $125, while food and other equipment cost as much again. For a total of $250 Rebell traveled for one year and eight days, a distance of over 8,000 nautical miles. As the boat and equipment were in good order and he still had $50 worth of food left on arrival in San Pedro, his total living and traveling expense for 373 days amounted to only $75.

Woman Alone
at Sea

by Clare Francis

MARCH, 1974

By the summer of 1973, five women had crossed the Atlantic alone. Clare Francis, 27, a sailor since childhood, wanted to be the sixth. The Englishwoman set out from Falmouth aboard a 32-foot Camper Nicholsons sloop; 37 days later she arrived in Newport.

This is not an ordinary logbook story of that crossing, but rather an introspective account of her anxieties, her rediscovery of music and friends, the techniques she used to fight self-pity, and the games she played with wind and sea.

Single-handers may be motivated by very different things, but once at sea they must face fairly similar psychological problems. Probably the most interesting of these are anxiety and loneliness. I say "anxiety" rather than "fear" because it is usually the anticipation of a dangerous event that is more difficult to bear than the event itself. Once the demon is upon you, it can be grappled with and overcome. Until then you live in a state of tension, wondering how and when it will strike, and whether you will be able to cope with it.

Of course, many of the dangers the single-hander faces are similar to those a fully crewed yacht may encounter, but the loner knows that she, and only she, can deal with the situation and that she must be prepared to do so at any time of the day or night, however exhausted she feels. It is a great challenge—but a lonely and worrying one.

Certainly my worst enemy was my imagination. As I set out from England to cross the Atlantic I was miserable with anxiety. I foresaw weeks of horror ahead; waves never less than twenty feet, ships bearing down on me while I slept in blissful ignorance below, and, most unpleasant to contemplate, the sight of the boat sailing off on her own as I bobbed around helplessly in the water. These thoughts continued to haunt me however hard I tried to think of more cheerful things (like the fun I was going to have when I arrived in Newport). But a week or so of the real thing did a lot to relieve my worries and to replace them with nothing worse than healthy anxiety. A gale is wet, bumpy, and extremely unpleasant at the best of times, but one is amazed to discover that one has seen steeper seas in the English Channel, that the wind isn't whistling as loudly as it did that time off Holland, and that, when one stops worrying, the boat rides the waves as well as she did before.

The first time I went through a gale single-handed, I was frozen to the cockpit for hours, watching with horrible fascination, as the seas became higher and higher. But thereafter I felt no more than nervous anticipation before a gale, excepting for one memorable occasion in the notorious Gulf Stream when the barometer took a dive, followed a few hours later by another one. My thoughts turned to hurricanes, and, having made all the necessary preparations, I began to await the worst. It was a cold, unpleasant kind of fear that crept up on me then, and it would have been marvelous to have someone to talk to, to joke with, to lift the tension. But when the gale finally came, it was such a relief to get to grips with it and so fascinating to observe (the seas were totally confused) that my fear soon evaporated.

Any worries I had about falling overboard soon diminished, too. I've always had good balance aboard boats, and there was no reason to think it would suddenly desert me now that I was alone in the middle of an ocean. Of course, I was always aware of the danger, and I'm sure I held on a bit tighter than I did in the company of other people. But I rarely wore a safety harness. I felt just as safe without one, unless the deck was performing particularly outrageous antics. Then I would clip myself to the lifelines as I moved around the deck. But what a nuisance it was. The line always became entangled around something at a critical moment.

No single-hander dares contemplate what she'd do if the worst actually occurred and she found herself in the water with the boat sailing off by itself. Under the peculiar circumstances of a lone voyage, one's love and appreciation of life become highly developed, and the possibility that it could all be snatched away in such a manner is just not acceptable. Any consideration of the event would be gruesome in the extreme.

The only anxiety that continued to bother me was that of being run down. One has so little defense against collision and, although my boat was positively bristling with radar reflectors and I showed a light every night, I would still wake up in a cold sweat and dash up on deck, fully expecting to see an enormous hull looming over me. My worries were refueled every time I saw a ship, for then I realized that the North Atlantic is not a large, empty place. It is extremely crowded.

One memorable day, when according to the Pilot Chart I was well off the shipping lanes, I saw three ships *simultaneously*. Under such circumstances it is very difficult to go below and sleep. When I first set out I would wake up every fifteen minutes or so, put my head up through the hatch and, sighing with relief at seeing no ships, try to grab some more rest. But as the passage continued, I began to sleep for an hour or more at a time. This is far too long if one is to sight a ship in time to get out of its way. It only takes fifteen minutes from the moment a ship appears over the horizon to the time it sinks you. Like many other single-handers, I had developed the "ostrich" syndrome. The mind gets tired of worrying, and it conveniently shuts off the moment you go down to the snug little world of the cabin. It's like a cocoon down there, and you feel secure and protected from the world outside, although you know such confidence has no rational basis.

Of course, ships don't constitute the only risk of collision. Whales and drifting timber or other jetsam are just as dangerous, if not more so, for you rarely have warning of their presence. But as time goes on, you become more philosophical and fatalistic about the whole thing, and from cold anxiety my feelings diminished to mild apprehension.

Oddly enough, the most obvious aspect of single-handing—the fact that one is alone—is not normally a major problem. Many single-handers feel moments of intense loneliness, but these rarely last long. The demanding business of sailing a small boat prevents the mind from dwelling on such undesirable emotions. Generally, a more positive feeling emerges. You think more about your family and friends and realize how lucky you are to have them. In the quiet moments, you become sentimental and nostalgic, and make all sorts of resolutions about how different things will be in the future. It's true for the single-hander—absence does make the heart grow fonder. But that absence is not unacceptable. In fact, it is almost pleasurable for the appreciation it engenders. I'm a sociable individual with a great fondness for the human race, and I found that being alone for thirty-seven days enhanced that feeling. But more, it made me resolve to be more tolerant and consider-ate of other people. And surprisingly, I remembered that resolution long after I stepped ashore. So this separation from the world can be a positive and constructive experience.

A long time alone is also a marvelous opportunity to indulge oneself in a great many pleasurable pastimes in a selfish way. One can sleep, read, write, or listen to music to the heart's content without fear of appearing antisocial. How I loved my books and my music (courtesy of a cassette player). They were like precious gifts, abandoned when I was a student and rediscovered now that I was away from the rush and tumble of city life. Putting the world to rights was also a favorite occupation of mine—there being no one to disagree with my brilliant theories for solving the world's problems, I never failed to find all the right answers. Thus, far from having difficulty in passing the time alone, I positively enjoyed the opportunities if offered. By the end of my voyage, my mind felt spring-cleaned and my soul rejuvenated.

However, I never felt entirely alone. One establishes a strong and personal relationship with one's closest companion, the boat. I was always chatting to *Gulliver G* about this and that. Either I congratulated her on our progress or commiserated with her when the elements conspired against us. And she always filled me with tremendous confi-dence. She was so strong and sturdy—and very much braver than I. But of course, far from being one's greatest ally, one's boat can become a liability. A leaking hull or a broken shroud can turn one's protector into something that has to be nursed and cared for, can turn a guardian angel into a sick friend. No longer can you leave her to ride out a gale while you rest below; she must be watched and worried over until the danger has passed. This imposes an almost unbearable strain on the single-hander, for then she is truly alone in the face of adversity.

The sea and the wind also became personalized to me. It is just you and them out there, and the three of you play a game of daring and cunning. It is a game. You shorten sail in expectation of a blow, but none comes—that's one point you award to the wind, minus one to you. You make two miles of progress in no more than a breath of wind against an uncomfortable swell—two points to you, minus one to the wind *and* the sea. And so on. I like to think that I'd won on points by the time I arrived in America. But although I warred with the elements in this way, I never thought of them as being overtly aggressive—just intolerant of mistakes. And much of the time they actually seemed friendly and benign, as if they were amused that I should venture out so far in such a small boat.

Many single-handers find that this contact with the elements extends itself to the essence of life, however you care to define that. Some find God; others converse with Father Neptune. Certainly I found strengths within myself I never knew were there. One way or another, being alone at sea for a long period of time is unlikely to make one *feel* alone. Like many others, I have found the isolation of living in a big city to be a much more devastating experience.

Of course, there were moments when I felt depressed and miserable, notably when setting out from England (what on earth was I *doing*?), when becalmed, or when pounding into strong headwinds for days on end. Calms were the ultimate in frustration. One seems to be making poor progress at the best of times, but when you have to sit for hours listening to the slam of the useless sails, knowing you're making little or no headway, it's almost too much to bear. And when, without steerage way, the boat would swing round to face the wrong direction—that was too much. Being alone, I found it difficult to accept such disappointments. It was a personal triumph for the wind and the sea against me. But as frustration is a very wearing emotion, I tried to take my mind off the situation by keeping busy.

Long periods of windward sailing also impose strains that can be hard to take. Prolonged crashing and pounding are tough on the nerves at the best of times, but when single-handed you cannot afford to sleep so deeply that you shut out all the noise. You must always have one ear open for any sound that suggests all is not well. As a result, I found I developed a kind of shell-shock. After a heavy crash of the bow I'd wake from my fitful sleep with a tremendous start, every nerve screaming, "Something must be broken this time." But it never was, so I'd try to sleep again. But, not knowing when the next crash was coming, my senses were alert, tense, and would permit no rest. If I dozed off, I would awaken suddenly, every nerve jangling in expectation that the next wave would crack the hull open. Rationally, I knew this wouldn't happen; but when you're tired, mentally and physically, danger seems to be very near.

It never failed to surprise me that my physical state could have the powerful effect on my psychological attitudes that it did. On a good day, when I felt rested and fit, my spirits were virtually uncrushable and it seemed that nothing could possibly go wrong. But after days and days of foul weather, little sleep, and a lot of physical exertion, it was difficult to see the bright side of life and I would crawl into my bunk, desolate and depressed, wondering what had possessed me to embark on such an awful venture.

But I never permitted myself the luxury of such self-pity for too long, partly as a matter of pride, but also because such emotions are destructive of energy and optimism which are vital to the single-hander if she is to keep ahead of the game. So whenever I felt low, I would give myself a morale booster in the form of a treat or a present. Such things took on an importance quite out of proportion to their normal significance. In particular, food was a great treat. My mother had given me a "Goodies Box" full of gorgeous and exotic foods like artichoke hearts, asparagus, candied chestnuts, honey, and chocolate. When I felt I deserved something from the Goodies Box, I would sit down like a small child with a box of candy and munch away until I felt better. Regular meals were also great events to be planned and looked forward to for hours beforehand. And I would never let the weather interfere with my meals, such was my anticipation of them. If I'd been looking forward to an omelette all day, then, dammit, come gale or storm, I was going to have one. And if the stove got covered with egg yolk which took days to burn off, well that was too bad. The important thing was the principle. One must never let the sea and the wind get the better of you.

My friends had given me a number of presents to open on the way across, and these became landmarks that I looked forward to for days. I had a "One Week Out Present" (several good books), a "Becalmed Present" (a jigsaw puzzle), a "Halfway Present" (a very funny tape recording made by my friends), a "Just Before Arrival Present" (a stick of deodorant), and many others. Those small gifts meant a lot to me. Not only did they raise my spirits, but they reminded me of how lucky I was to have such good friends.

Quite ordinary events also became high spots of the day—having a wash in fresh water, putting on clean clothes, listening to my favorite tape. All of these things counteracted the disappointments and frustrations I experienced, not only from the weather or lack of progress but from the myriad small things that can so easily get you down. A leak over your bunk, wet bedding, wet clothes, an irreplaceable engine part lost in the bilge, a bruised back, lack of sleep, an aching head—the list is endless. But all of these minor pitfalls had to be overcome. I found it essential to "think positive" at all times, for then I was able to master any situation *and* be ready for the next.

There were many chores that, given half a chance, I would put off tackling for hours. A ruthless kind of lethargy would creep up on me, and I would find any number of reasons for reading or sleeping instead of tidying the cabin, scrubbing the galley, oiling the winches. I found I had to mount what I called an "anti-vegetation campaign" every day to get things done. Even writing up the log was a task that I tried to put off to the evening, when I was generally too tired to make a good job of it.

But there were two chores I always accomplished immediately. One was sail changing. If I had too much sail up, I was so nervous that something would break that I would shorten sail as soon as possible. If too little sail, I so hated to feel the boat going at less than her best that I would hurry to press more sail on. Navigation was the other task I never put off. The excitement of finding out how much progress I'd actually made against my dead reckoning was important, as was the game of getting halfway, two-thirds the way, seven-eighths the way across. If I arrived at my target sooner than I'd hoped, it was one point to me; if later, then it was one point again to the wind and the sea.

So, as a single-hander one lives largely from moment to moment, meeting each new task or situation as best one can. It is a psychological exercise of some magnitude to identify the problems that emanate both from the sea and from within oneself, then to face them and solve them—entirely alone. The satisfaction from so doing is deep satisfaction indeed.

Captain Jim
and *Reynard*

by *Marjorie Young Burgess*

FEBRUARY, 1947

So *Reynard* has gone. A single statement in a Rhode Island newspaper after the last hurricane gave the clue: "Also lost was the old catboat *Reynard*, which slipped her mooring and was pounded to pieces on the seawall." I did not need the more accurate confirmation later naming "the fifty-year-old sloop *Reynard*." She had so often been miscalled "that old catboat" that I recognized her instantly.

Judged by modern standards she was a brute, 40 feet on deck, 11 feet beam, centerboard, about 700 square feet in her gaff mainsail on a long overhanging boom, and about 200 more in the jib on the end of a 6-foot bowsprit. The racing men were none too respectful, but there was something to her style, something about the big, deep oval cockpit with the high coamings, something about the wide old-fashioned stern that made her homelike and comfortable. If you cruised on her, you loved her and, as if she were your grandmother, resented comment on her figure.

She could not take two hurricanes at her age. The one in 1938 almost finished her, but Captain Jim Currier coaxed her back to life. She was not as spry as she had been, and Captain Jim said he would never again take her outside Narragansett Bay after she had gone ashore and been patched up. She had one more summer with him as her skipper before he, too, slipped his mooring. She waited for the next hurricane, but it was really the first that took them both.

She was my school ship, so to speak, for I learned about cruising from her—to hold a straight course and lay out the next, to choose the snuggest anchorage and belay the halliards before turning in, to put away a big breakfast and be ravenous for the next meal, as well as the joys of being dunked from a bowsprit, and the delicious lameness that comes of throwing your whole body into hauling up 700 square feet of mainsail, or trimming it in with a fist-filling mainsheet, and how to relax when someone else is on watch, stretching like a cat and listening to the water slip past her seamy old sides.

She had more than cruising to teach. I saw her first when she was only 40, one wintry day with a great hole gaping in her bottom where the centerboard trunk had been pulled out to make way for new timbers. Before next spring, I knew her through and through—from her linen locker and hard bunks in the forecastle to her marline-smelling lazarette aft between icebox and transom. And I had learned to drill holes two feet long in a straight line, to find her deck beams with a nail from topside when we renailed the whole deck, to slobber canvas and myself with white lead when we recovered the deck, to run a drill press when we made the bolt holes in the bronze rudder stock, to sharpen a plane when we smoothed up the three-inch oak planks of her new barn-door rudder, and to swing pick and shovel when the time came to hang it in place. Then as the warmth of summer drew near and we established a stopping point in our work, I learned the pride that comes when you sweep up the shavings, scrub down the deck, and polish up the brass, for the snowy canvas must lie in spotless cleanliness while the age-old business of bending sail takes place, with marline seizing it to the hoops and lace lines running along gaff and boom, then the first furl when the heavy canvas is soft as linen and begging for the breeze. Life begins at 40, the tale goes, and she was frisky as a kitten with all the good, sound new wood and the loving care we had put into her.

Captain Jim had promised the working crew the first cruise, on which we set out late one soft warm day in early June. The weather had been fair for six weeks, and we had made the most of it. The first cruise after two years ashore was taking place on schedule. The little scudding black cotton clouds around the horizon only amused us. What matter if it should rain? We had done the work before the weekend and had that Friday night and the two following whole days. Where to go?

Captain Jim and his daughter Carolyn chose Potter's Cove on Prudence Island, and promised the rest of us—Harry, Joe, and myself— the most perfect of anchorages when we should arrive. So high were our spirits as we imagined the following weekends of the summer spent in just this way that we would have been content to go just across the bay to Jamestown.

We had a leisurely sail up the bay with a southwest wind over the port quarter, and hauled up on the wind for only the short entrance to the harbor. Then our first meal on board, and our delighted discovery of the miraculous amount of food that thin young Harry could hold, and the astounding combinations of food that appealed to him. Meals were always happy on *Reynard*, if for no other reason than that one had only to catch Harry's eye in the middle of one, and first he and then the whole crew around the big oak table would become convulsed with laughter.

Perhaps we were too gay. We did not then have the proper caution desirable in sailors. We turned in at about 10 o'clock, drowsy as only one can be after a sail, and it was 4 a.m. before the first one awakened. I awoke because my right ear was full of water, my pillow was sopped, and the stream running down the middle of the mattress had just reached my shoulderblade. Rain was drumming overhead. Though we had canvassed her deck and painted her inside and out, we had not gotten around to the seams in the cabin top that had stood uncovered in the hot sun for six weeks on a boat that had not been in the water for two years.

Someone lit a flashlight. Harry, his eyes screwed tightly shut, threw back a blanket and raised his sleepy head, still adorned with his new yachting cap. There was little sleep after that. In fact, there was little sleep the rest of the weekend, for the rain did not stop until Sunday afternoon. We sat on bottom-up saucepans and played with wet cards on the dripping table. We swam in the rain, we rowed in the rain, we hiked in the rain, and we ate well-watered meals.

Sunday afternoon we sailed back down the bay to Newport in a thick fog. It was still fun, and it was a good sail. We forgave *Reynard*, caulked and painted the cabin top, and had our other weekends. Never again did we experience such a wetting. She proudly drew her planks together in the dampness and kept us dry thereafter, relatively speaking.

She had had many such summers before, but that was my first cruising season. A lot of its pleasure sticks with me still.

Captain Jim Currier was chief ordnance engineer of the naval torpedo station in Newport, Rhode Island, and in those days could get away on Friday afternoons. His crew would do the provisioning, fill up the icebox, replenish the water bottle from a spring in the country, and be ready to start the instant he appeared. Each weekend saw *Reynard* in some different harbor of the bay, until August when the peak of the season, the two weeks' cruise, took place.

There were six of us for that cruise, Captain Jim, his wife, their daughters Cons and Carolyn, Harry and I, invading what was to me the virgin cruising ground of Nantucket, Martha's Vineyard, and the Elizabeth Islands, though it was an old story to *Reynard*, these being scenes of many previous holidays.

There were many highlights of the cruise—sailing with full sweep of the tide through Wood's Hole, the "wild horses" of Naushon, the gloriously wet roaring sail across the shoals to Nantucket, the deliciously warm waters of Nantucket Harbor; the choppy pounding beat back to Hadley's Harbor, the grounding on Onset at just the moment I said, "Here, you take her. I don't want to be the one to put her aground." We bent the centerboard on that one and added another job to the list for the winter.

My strongest memory of the cruise is of my first all-night sail from Marion to Wickford, beating down Buzzards Bay with a fresh breeze that got lighter as the full moon sank deeper and deeper into the cloudy fog. About midnight we caught Mischaum light over our stern, due north, just as the fog shut down. The sleepy watch on deck grew less and less alert. The skipper was wrapped in drowsy peace at the wheel, with wind almost imperceptible and *Reynard* ghosting along in the blackness. Suddenly I leaped fully awake from the hardness of the cockpit seat where I lay.

"I smell bayberry bushes!" At just that moment Captain Jim caught the sound of ripples on a beach close aboard. Hard over in that instant went the wheel, over with the surge went the boom and gaff, and down on the cabin sole with a thud rolled the occupants off both port bunks. We dared sail only north to get clear, as we had come. A quick look at the chart showed us that *Reynard* had silently led us into the safety of Robinson's Hole between two islands. Once clear of the land we found the breeze again and shortly picked up the nearest buoy to lay our course for Hen and Chickens lightship.

The breeze was fine once more, and we were close hauled to starboard, passing close aboard the lightship, when we sighted the running lights of a small freighter who threw her impersonal spotlight on us in passing. For an instant we were lifted out of the black void, the sounds of the box wave had another dimension as we saw the white water tossed off to port; the sail, unperceived in the darkness, now towered startlingly above us. We were as self-conscious as if from the vault of heaven the Author of the universe had turned the light of his searching eye down on us alone.

It was gone in a flash. We had a snack all round and changed watches. Heavy-lidded and achingly tired, I stretched out on some wadded blankets to leeward in Stateroom A, the forecastle, and never knew whether I slept or not, so pleasant was the sensation of being cradled in the upsurge of the bow, lightly tossed at the crest of a wave, then gently caught and cradled once more as the bow swept on and down to meet the next upswing. For hours *Reynard* held to this angle of heel and this course, and brought us at dawn to Sakonnet Point.

At Wickford that noon we had a Roman feast, with the choicest of seagoing desserts, watermelon, after which all hands instantly collapsed and slept for several hours. *Reynard* taught us one lesson with her all-night sail. It is a wonderful thing to have done once.

As eventually happens in all cruising, the end of summer arrived. Once more the boat was laid up and worked on, scraped, sanded, and painted. Once more Captain Jim removed the parts he wanted to repair and took them to his workshop cellar. All the crews of the previous summer gathered in the dusty workshop to sand and paint or sit and talk. For Captain Jim was a man who used his hands as well as he used his head. It was a pleasure and an education to pitch in and help him. He had done likewise for all of us. When a new dory was added to our small-boat racing fleet, he was the one who made the bronze tangs, who refitted the rudder with bronze gudgeons and pins of his own fashioning, who showed us how to splice our wire rigging, who made us light racing booms with perfect little outhauls, who adjusted our centerboard pins, and whose own home-built trailer was used to haul and launch the little fleet. He was the heart and spirit of the yacht club, the racing and the cruising, and after he went it was never the same.

When I left the yacht club, the racing, and the *Reynard* cruising to labor in the world, my younger sister inherited my berth on *Reynard*, and wrote me of cruises up the bay and around to Third Beach and the Sakonnet River, while I pictured her learning of boats and growing happier and wiser in the ways of the sea. She will remember her first long cruise as I did mine, though in a quite different way.

The summer of '38 had passed with no cruise of any length. Small-boat racing on weekends, engrossing the crew, and increasing pressure of work at the torpedo station had kept the old vessel close to her mooring. She had gone out on many a summer evening when a willing crew was mustered to take her across the harbor and out into the channel, perhaps to the lightship off Brenton's Reef where the sea breezes play at night, loath to approach the land. Then before the weakening breeze she would ghost homeward, barely carrying steerage way as she lost the last zephyr to come out of Brenton's Cove, and would nestle to her mooring in the glassy black mirror in the leeward corner of the harbor. Her sleepy crew would snug her down for the rest of the night and row ashore, damp, tired, and happy.

Or perhaps on that summer, as on so many others, when the sun had heated the land and the houses ashore to an oven-like temperature, *Reynard* would bear a crew of six across the harbor to anchor in Brenton's Cove and sleep under blankets and awaken to fresh energies in the morning. Midget cruises, these, which left the crew eager for a longer and more memory-enduring one.

The weather was foul later that summer, and one thing and another interfered until the anticipated cruise to Buzzards Bay or Long Island Sound had been postponed several times. At last in mid-September, after a week of rainy weather, it was decided to seize the first good day (surely the harbinger of fair weather to follow) and set out. At last one such day arrived. The overcast sky began to clear, patches of blue to appear, and the spirits of the restless crew to rise. They did the last bit of provisioning, filled the icebox, and got under way late in the morning. The crew on this memorable voyage were Captain Jim's 22-year-old son

Jimmie, his friend Bill of the same age, and two younger girls, Emily, 19, and my sister Connie, 17.

As the weather was still far from settled, Captain Jim decided to take his crew up the bay rather than out to sea, and tucked a double reef into the mainsail, standard procedure in the face of strong winds. They dropped the mooring in the shelter of Newport Harbor, swung around Long Wharf, and headed for the channel between Gull Rock and the Naval War College.

Once out of the shadow of the land, they felt the force of the easterly wind, coming in quick and increasingly heavy gusts. Captain Jim knew immediately that they were in for a real sail, and that there was no turning back. On they leaped, with heavy blasts of beam wind off the easterly shore driving the old vessel through churning seas and heeling her unmercifully. Captain Jim froze to the wheel, staring grimly ahead, hands gripping the spokes, and impressing his young crew with the force of his will to bring his vessel through. Up the bay they charged. The kerosene for the lamps was the first casualty. A five-gallon bottle was thrown across the cockpit, broke, and flooded the bilge with the foul-smelling stuff. The crew was silent. Few orders were given by the rigid man at the wheel, and few were needed. Each watched anxiously for the moment when he or she could be most useful. Jimmie was of course second in command and stood ready for emergency. It soon came. The jib, strained beyond further endurance, blew out of its hooks, and Jimmie and Bill made the remnants fast as best they could.

By now they were approaching Melville, then a naval coaling station with docks but no harbor. Captain Jim told them that he was going to try to work up into the lee and make fast to the dock. The elements refused to permit him. *Reynard* tried valiantly to bring her bow to the wind, but her mainsail, with a sickening sound, ripped from leech to luff. Some men on the dock shouted unintelligibly down the whipping wind, the crew waved in a comradely way, and *Reynard* tore past, Captain Jim sticking grimly to his wheel, Jimmie and Bill working to secure the slatting gaff and peak of the mainsail. Connie was stationed aft beside Captain Jim to sit on the canvas that dripped from the boom and thus provided a scrap of sail. Once the gaff was lashed down, Bill also came aft to sit on the deck with feet over the transom and shove mightily on the nose of the Dyer dink when she surged forward on the seas to dash her stem against *Reynard*'s counter.

The young crew was soaked, hungry, tired, and scared, but Connie said later that the strong figure of Captain Jim at the wheel kept their confidence high. Now and then he would issue a brief order, the details of execution to be worked out by Jimmie. For once he was not interested in the one right way of doing something. Just let it be done. I can see him, too, bending aside to shout a brief remark designed to keep up the spirits of those youngsters under his care, but for the most part the responsibility of getting his ship and the lives aboard her safely into harbor weighed heavily on him. The confidence of my worried parents was a tribute. Through all this day and the following night they did not despair of Connie's safety, assuring each other that with Mr. Currier she must be safe.

Wind and seas were worse as they left the lee of the land and bore off for the north end of Prudence Island. They were dead before the easterly now with only a rag of sail. *Reynard* lumbered with the dinghy constantly trying to ram through her transom. Somehow they managed to dig out the "insurance," the 175-pound anchor under the icebox beneath the cockpit, and secure it forward, and to make ready the heavy reserve rode. The tension eased as they neared Potter's Cove, the little land-locked harbor whose bush covered sandbar curves like a protecting arm around from the north to intercept the easterly winds and seas.

Steadily seas and wind increased, but *Reynard* swung gratefully around the bar and into the empty little harbor. Over went the anchors, the light one and the "insurance." Only then did Captain Jim relax, after he had gone forward to inspect the rodes on the bitts. "Safe at last," he said.

All hands were hungry and sat munching in the cockpit while the wind screamed over them. They pumped the kerosene out of the bilge and put the cabin to rights, then settled down to watch the sea rise and gradually eat away the flat bit of land that spelled safety for the tired old vessel. Up the water crept, cutting the little stretch of sand and bush back and back until it was evident there would soon be no kindly barrier, no shelter whatever from the howling shrieking winds and the merciless seas dashing themselves against the sand and casting their spray tops to the wind. There were several hours of watching and awaiting the inevitable. Then, after the last of the land had crumbled before the onslaught of the waves, *Reynard* began her slow drag to shore.

She was caught on a lee shore, pinned with no chance to escape, no sail, and a roaring, driving hurricane of wind beating her inexorably to a dread hard resting place and destruction ashore. What despair must have filled Captain Jim as he watched the slow shoreward movement as the pitching bows dragged his anchors along, with all the windage of the old gaff-rigged boat aiding the destruction. His thoughts were first for his crew and how best to protect them when she struck. For himself he must have had doubts, for he had a game leg. Infantile paralysis had left one foot paralyzed, and he was a heavy man for others to help. "You must each look out for yourselves," he told his four young companions.

The dinghy had long since parted her painter and vanished downwind into the flying mist. They could no longer even attempt to look into the wind, which picked up salt spray and tried to drive it through them.

The strain of waiting was lightened by Bill's irrepressible Bob Hope-like sense of humor which suffered no pause, unless it was when he begged Captain Jim to allow him to swim ashore with a rope tied to his waist on which the others might pull themselves to safety. Captain Jim would have none of it.

As they approached the land, they took stock of the situation. *Reynard*, shallow with board up, would get very close before striking. The land to leeward was once a sandy bluff about thirty feet high with marshland at its foot. Only the bluff now showed. When they were quite close, they tried to salvage all the articles possible. To the boys' delight they found that all they needed to do was throw things straight in the air, for the wind would whip them ashore.

At last *Reynard* grounded and swung broadside to the wind and the surges at the foot of the bluff whose bush-covered top was halfway up the mast. The poor ship rolled slowly and heavily in the wash and backwash, heeling to the wind, then pounding her leeward bilge with a thud into the muddy bank and sending up a geyser of mud and water between boat and bank.

Connie, being the youngest and but newly awakened to the dubious joys of sailing, was the first ashore. She stood on the gaff clutching the halliard. As *Reynard* took her toll to shore, the boys heaved. Up she went, grabbed for a bush, and scrambled to the top. Here she tried to look back and help Emily, but could not face the wind, let alone open her eyes into it. She could barely crouch, as the force of the wind rolled her again and again into the bushes. Suddenly, over the roar of wind and crash of the boat's side against shore, she heard a scream. Moments later Emily, almost unrecognizable so plastered with mud, came over the bank, dripping. She had slipped and fallen overboard between the boat and the bank. As she fell, one hand caught the gunwale, and Bill, who was nearest, with a single perfect motion, yanked her back to the deck before the boat completed her roll into the mud.

Captain Jim was next, I do not see how, and after him the two boys. They collected the clothing they had heaved to shore and set out across the fields for shelter. A kindly couple, who had watched *Reynard* sweep into the cove, received them and put them up for the sleepless night.

Early the next morning, on a clear blue sunny day, they went back to look for the wreckage. High and dry, several hundred feet from the bluff and from the beach lay *Reynard* on her side, half full of sand and mud, trunk cabin ripped from her deck on one side, and a shambles on deck and below. Jimmie said that the sight was almost too much for him. Over and over through his head hammered the thought, "My father's boat! My father's boat!"

She was in sorry condition, but Jimmie elected to live aboard her, clean her out, and protect her from scavengers until his father could get back to the mainland and investigate salvage possibilities. His Robinson Crusoe life lasted about two weeks before the rescue party arrived.

The comradeship of boats and boatmen is a wonderful thing. Many a power boatman at the club had sniffed his disapproval of "that old box." They could not understand why her crew loved her so on even the calmest days when she could go nowhere, being without power, and many of them could not understand the pleasure in going out for an evening's sail and barely getting back in the small hours of the morning. But they understood a boat and a good skipper in trouble, and turned to. Even the Navy helped. Early that Saturday morning there chugged into Potter's Cove a torpedo station range boat with two sailors to handle her, and about thirty men from the yacht club armed with spades, tackle, and food. They dug manfully around the boat, improvised a railway, dragged her down to the beach, floated her, towed her home, pumping, and made a game of it.

That winter the little cellar workshop was again filled with shavings. At the end of the evening pieces of mellowed and well-salted wood went once more into the living room fireplace while old burning copper paint made rich green and blue plumes in the flames for resting workers to watch and remember. Once more blocks of new wood were pulled out and examined before being declared fit to go into *Reynard*.

I missed that winter's work, and I missed, too, the summer that followed, when *Reynard* was not allowed by Captain Jim to go out of the bay. She had been strained, and might not stand more such punishment. Perhaps Captain Jim realized, too, that his strain had been great, but he never mentioned it. When the sailing summer was over and *Reynard* hauled out, one day as he sat working on the floor with his tools around him, his life ran out and he was gone.

Jimmie dreamed a night or so later that his father came to life for a short space to direct his own funeral, as what skipper would not lay out for his crew the necessary preparations for the longest cruise of all.

Without Captain Jim, *Reynard* was restive. He had recalled her to life when she lay exhausted on the sands, had painfully dragged her back to the water. She missed him keenly the first summer that he was gone. Young Jim was skipper now, but the cruises were not the same. One weekend she almost piled herself up on Halfway Rock in a dense fog. A startled skipper and crew saw the rock go by in the fog barely twenty feet abeam when they had reckoned on a wide berth. Perhaps she could not quite bring herself to risk their lives again.

Young Jim parted with her reluctantly that fall. He felt that things were too different aboard, and sold her up the bay. I almost lost touch with her then. At one time I heard that she had a motor installed and was at East Greenwich.

I was at Quonset Point Naval Air Station in 1944 when the next hurricane roared up Narragansett Bay, and my thoughts were constantly going back to that previous adventure I had missed. As I tried to sleep that night in the Waves' quarters, riding in on the wind was the vision of that mad sail up the bay and the granite will of Captain Jim to save his boat. It was not until later that I read in the newspapers that *Reynard* had been dashed to pieces on the seawall of the Rhode Island Yacht Club.

She went completely this time, and now her timbers and planks are a part of the ebb and flow of the bay where her life was led. Somehow I think that is what has happened to Captain Jim, too.

2

The Passion of
Thomas Fleming Day

Thomas Fleming Day, Rudder's first editor, hit yachting like an unexpected jibe.

Railing against what he called "the rocking chair fleet," he set out to sea in small boats, reveling in the ocean's gales and mocking the wails from the shore crowd which predicted his demise. He initiated deep-water racing in 1904 with a competition between New York and Marblehead, Massachusetts. He organized the first Bermuda race in 1906, entered it, and won. He printed designs of small boats, told readers step by step how to build from the plans, built the boats himself, and trusted his life to them in long voyages.

Those who knew Day reported that he was a quiet, pipe-smoking man with short curly hair, a moustache, and penetrating eyes. He was a good salesman, and started Rudder *in 1890 in part as an advertising medium for the skiffs he sold at the New York City showroom of J. J. Bockee & Co.*

The first issues, published at Bockee's, had a homey flavor. "We come to gossip and chat with you," Day told his readers in Number 1 of Volume I. But after a few years, Day's prose became biting and fearless. His column "Round the Clubhouse Fire"—from which the following excerpts were taken—often singed the complacent clubhouse set. It was Day's passion to get them all off their duffs and onto the water in boats, where he himself had found adventure and joy.

On Writers

DECEMBER, 1902

Having been writing yarns steadily for about three weeks, I am thoroughly pen-sick, and would be deuced glad to chuck that instrument into the fire and follow it with the inkpot and pad of paper. Some old idiot—I don't remember now whether it was Dr. Johnson or Chelsea Carlisle—went into panegyrics over the individual who invented books. For my part, I believe that man to have been the greatest enemy of his race that ever blew breath, and to have deserved hanging instead of praise. Anyhow, as that may be, at least nine-tenths of the people who publish books ought to be married to the ropemaker's daughter for encouraging the making of such pestiferous things. If the devil had set Job to writing a novel, the old Hebrew would have knocked under at the third round. I often sit here and look at the fleet of fifty-odd volumes harbored in one of the bookcases, all by one man, and wonder what kind of writing machine that cuss was. He must have done nothing but write from the time he left the cradle until the doctors finished him off. Just think of a man wasting his life in that way. Thank goodness, we've got more use for the days that are given us! I don't believe the Creator intended man for any such purpose, and every year become more firmly convinced that writing is a form of insanity, and that all authors are what the brain experts call degenerates. I don't know exactly what that term defines, but I suppose it must be the proper one, because everybody uses it nowadays. Talking is different; man was created to talk. He was born with a tongue, and nature prompts him to use it. Despite the sayings of countless philosophers, who through all ages have inveighed against loose speech, I'm of the opinion that a man who constantly keeps his mouth shut is a stupid ass. Although thousands have captured a reputation for wisdom in this way, and gone down to posterity as wise and learned because they talked not, there is no reason why we should remain tongue-tied. Let no such reputation straddle our graves. So here's to the talking man, long may he live, and be with us to enjoy our company and our fire.

A Day Lexicon

FEBRUARY, 1901

Several men have been bothering me lately, wanting to know which phrase is correct: "to way anchor," or "to weigh anchor." This is old yarn that has been spun over, time and time again, and has generally been balled-up wrongly by the wiseacres who turned the winch. These self-created authorities have quoted from several dictionaries to prove their assertions, not for one moment suspecting that the man who made the lexicon knew as little about what he was doing as they did when repeating his misstatements. If you want to ascertain the purity of a water flowing from a spring, it is no use to sample it a mile from the source; the place to get your beakerful is at the fountainhead. So it is with nautical terms. Go back to the morning hours of language, wise one. It is simply absurd to hold, as some lexicon-makers do, that those who created and first used these terms did not know what they meant to mean. The man who first called a spade a spade certainly knew that he meant the term to describe a spade, and not a hoe. Now if the learned gentlemen who make lexicons had taken the trouble to look up the

writings of the old and original seamen, they would have discovered that
the verb-phrase *to way*, meaning to raise the anchor, and *to weigh*,
meaning to measure the force of gravity, are totally different terms.
Weigh, to measure gravity, was originally spelled *waye*, and is so
spelled in old state papers of the time of Henry of much-married
memory. At the same time, and in the following reigns of Elizabeth and
James I, the word *way*, meaning to raise the anchor, is spelled *way*, and
is unquestionably an abbreviation of the word *sway*, the original order
probably being to *sway* the anchor. The first dictionary-makers, like
Philips, Blount, and Johnson, who probably knew as much about
Chinamen and elephants as they did about ships and seamen, consequently confused the two words, owing to their having the same sound,
and then somebody decided to spell it *weigh*. In those good old days,
when dictionaries and spelling books were scarce, every man was his
own Josh Billings, and might spell the same word three different ways
on the same page without being brought to book, as there was no book to
bring him to. This is especially so of nautical terms, as, aside from the
list made in the time of Charles I and held in the archives of the
Admiralty, there was no compilation until Falconer undertook the task,
some hundred years later. As to which is correct, there is no question—
''to way anchor,'' is the proper phrase. If you do not believe that I know
what I am talking about, allow me to refer you to the narratives of
North-West Fox, Smith, Frobisher, or any of the worthies who sailed
and sought unknown lands in the time of Mary and Bess. Some of these
tales you will find in the never worn out Hakluyt, but mind you are to
read them in the early editions, and not when modernized and partly
spoiled. After listening to the above, you will probably slam down the
sheet and exclaim, ''What a lot that fellow thinks he knows!'' Well, he
does know about some things, and ought to, for he has been doing
nothing else all his life but reading and reasoning. One thing my
explorations in this particular direction have taught me, and that is, a
contempt for two classes of scholars—the grammarian and lexicon
tinker. Both have done their best to defile and distort the noblest
language that ever rolled from the tongue of man. Its symmetry and
purity have only been saved for us by the singing of the master poets. It
was Chaucer, Spenser, Shakespeare, and Milton who conceived, built,
deepened, and beautified our speech; it is men like Johnson, Todd,
Webster, and their kind who have marred and mauled it.

DECEMBER, 1904

A number of people have asked me at different times about the word "port," as used to designate the left-hand side of a vessel. It seems that lately there has been printed in the magazines a lot of nonsensical stories about Paul Jones, written by people who have little or no knowledge of the sea and less of the art of writing. In one of these, the celebrated renegade is made to send his men to man the *port battery*, and he also orders them to fire a *port broadside*. Now, in the time of Jones, the word port was not used to designate the left-hand side, and it is very unlikely that Paul ever mouthed any such order. What he did say was, "Man the larboard guns!" The word larboard was generally used until the early part of the nineteenth century, both in the naval and merchant marine; it is still somewhat employed, I understand, on the Great Lakes and western rivers. If you notice the hatch covers on a ship, you will find those for the port side marked "L." A friend, captain of a steamer, once asked the carpenter, who was laboriously carving an L on the hatch, why he marked the cover in that way. He did not know why, he said, but it was the custom to do so. The use of this mark has survived the word it once belonged to—larboard. Possibly the ease of cutting an L has helped to keep it alive.

Of course, sailors soon found that the words larboard and starboard, owing to the similarity of sound, were apt to be mistaken, and lead to trouble; but it was centuries before they changed things. One reason for this was that in the early days the helmsman was the pilot, just as the skipper of a small coasting vessel steers his own ship. Therefore, it was not necessary to give helm orders, as the steersman had only to whisper in his own ear what to do. But when vessels grew big and became regular men-o'-war that had to be commanded by officers, the confusion of larboard and starboard manifested. The earliest reference I find to the use of the word port is in an account of a conflict between an Algerian Corsair and an English merchant off the chops of the channel. In this the English master orders the steersman to put the helm a-port, so as to sheer off from the rover and prevent her boarding him. This, if I remember rightly, happened in the reign of James II. The word port is derived from the same term used in pike drill, in which one of the orders is "pikes a-port"—that is, to hold the pike staff diagonally across the body, same as port a musket in our old manual of arms. It was used originally aboard a vessel as an order to the helmsman to put the helm hard over either way; in other words, port the tiller across the helmsman's body, just as he would a pike in drill. When it became customary to con a helm to larboard and starboard, the phrase a-port was substituted for a-larboard, but it does not seem to have come into common use until late in the eighteenth century, as you frequently find letters from naval and merchant skippers suggesting its employment. In many accounts of actions and accidents, the word larboard is used down to about 1800. About 1840 the Admiralty issued an order that thereafter on all the H.M. ships the word port was to designate the left-hand side of a vessel, in place of the term larboard. Its use died out later in the merchant marine, but even in my early days old seamen still spoke of the larboard side.

FEBRUARY, 1906

An inquiry from a gentleman asks what authority there is for using the word "beam" to designate the width of a vessel. There is no authority; the proper term is breadth. The use of the term beam in place of breadth seems to have come in through the ignorance of half-educated persons writing about yachting. It cannot be found anywhere but in yachting literature. The term is not and never was used by shipbuilders. I have searched Mungo Murray, Charnock, Sutherland, Partington, and others, and they always use the term breadth. It is also invariably used in all government papers and by all writers on shipping. The use of the word beam probably arose in this way. In the old days the measurement for tonnage was the length of the keel multiplied by the *breadth at the main beam*. In speaking of a vessel in one of his papers, Sir Walter Raleigh said she was so many feet "breadth of the main beam." Now it is likely that a man wanting to know the size of another man's vessel would ask "what is your main beam?" meaning what is the width of your ship at the main beam. This inquiry was gradually shortened to "breadth of beam" and at last to "beam." The word first appears in this sense in literature about fifty years ago. I have used it and sometimes from carelessness still use it, but it is unquestionably incorrect.

On the Rules
of the Road

OCTOBER, 1900, and DECEMBER, 1909

Take one night off a week this winter and spend it studying the Rules of
the Road. It is shameful and scandalous that men who know nothing at
all about these rules should go on the water in charge of boats. What
would you think of a man who started to drive a carriage or an auto who
did not know which side of the road to take in meeting another vehicle?
A man with average intelligence can learn these rules in a week. I wish
the clubs would take the matter up, for unless something is done, the
government will be forced to take drastic action. I append a clipping
containing some remarks by Captain J. A. Thompson of the Metropoli-
tan Line turbine *Yale*:

> "The navigator of the Sound is rejoicing over the closing of
> the excursion season. He never has been hampered so much as he
> has this last summer by motor boats that on Sundays and public

holidays swarm in the sea space between Hell Gate and Execution Rock. To appreciate the hazard that has been added to the perils of steamboating in the Sound a man should take a trip on a pleasant Sunday and make observations from the pilot house or near it. None, or mighty few of the men who run motor boats, know the significance of whistles. I used to give them the signal to go starboard or port, whichever happened to be the safest course for my command and the motor boats. They simply did not know why I was signaling. Now I just go ahead and dodge them. There are so many of them that it is a waste of steam to whistle, and I slow down and thread my way through the jam. It is a wonder that there are not more of them run down. I dread them more than I do the densest fog on the Sound."

Three times this summer I myself have been obliged to give way at the last moment in order to prevent a collision, almost brought about by an utter disregard of the rule that a boat on a wind on the starboard tack has the right of way. It is certain that in one case the man helming the other boat knew that he was in the wrong; in the other the skippers most likely did not know which tack they were on. A large yawl, running with the wind on her beam, forced me round, we tacking just in time to avert a collision. In response to my protest I was requested by the skipper to go to a place not on the map. There was no excuse for his conduct, as he had plenty of water on both sides, and was in no way hampered by my course. Similar pigheadedness on the part of a coaster captain in the Shoals this summer resulted in a bad foul between two schooners and the loss of a life. The danger in trying to weather a man when on the wrong tack is this: He, knowing he is in the right, will stand on, expecting the other boat to obey the rule and keep off or tack. At the last moment, fearful of a foul, he will put up his helm to save himself, and as likely as not the man on the port tack will do the same—the result, a collision. The offenders in almost all cases are larger vessels. Now, a small vessel has the same rights, and the same obligations, as a large vessel. She is not justified in parting with the former or ignoring the latter. If she give way when in the right, and a foul ensue, she has no redress. In order to insure safety, all vessels, small and large, must live up to every word of the code. But this is impossible, you will say. It *is* as things now are; but if a law were passed enabling a vessel forced out of her right to report the offending craft and have a fine imposed, it would soon alter the case. As it is, you have no redress, unless there is actual damage, and then only for the amount of damage done. The risk of life is not considered by the courts.

It certainly is rather a strain on one's faculties to come to the belief that there are men handling yachts who do not know when they are on the right tack. But it is truthfully so. I have known men who have knocked about in the water for years who could not with certainty tell whether they were on the port or starboard tack. They were as a class just as ignorant in other things. Some of them had never heard of the Rules of the Road; others had never read them. Many yacht skippers cannot read a chart, and very few of them have more than a superficial knowledge of the compass! I was told of one this summer who brought out his compass and stood it on an iron pig. When asked if the metal would affect the instrument, he answered that it never did, and wound up by declaring that "the thing was no good, anyhow," and that in sailing at night or in fog "he'd rather trust to what he knowed." Half the yachtsmen I meet have no knowledge of a compass. They know nothing of variation or deviation and cannot tell whether the compass is right or wrong. Very few know how to correct the instrument or to take bearings with it, or to do anything except steer just as she points. You will generally find that men of this type are those who have a contempt for books and all class of reading that brings knowledge. They are too ignorant to know that they are ignorant. Imagine a man being an officer of a club who does not know the names of the four corners of a sail. You don't have to imagine it, for the person lives, and, what is worse, talks. In one of his lectures he informed me that he had no use for yachting publications, "as they couldn't learn him nothing"—a statement that at once I gladly admitted to be a fact, much to his pleasure. Such a man is to be pitied, but the organization that put the stars on his cap ought to be inoculated with syrup of fitness.

On Cooks

MARCH, 1906

Talking about the cook, we need several to go in the ocean race. Navigators are to be had in plenty, but cooks are scarce as poets. In the old days in the British Navy, the cook was a person of considerable importance, he being the last officer to leave the ship when she went out of commission; consequently, at sunset it was his duty to haul down the pendant. So long as the pendant was flying, although paid off, the officers and crew were not allowed to leave the boundaries of the port. One day a seventy-four was paid off and the crew anxious to be away watched for the pendant to come down, but sunset came and it still flew. Cook was missing. Instantly orders were sent up for a general chase and the town was thoroughly scoured. At last after some hours the man of pots and kettles was found self-stewed, taken aboard ship, and made to haul down the whip. Why are good cooks nearly always drunkards? Only answer to that is another question. Did you ever know a really good sea cook? Anyhow, the Board of Trade has established a sea-cook school in London, and that is the most sensible thing it has ever done. Bad cooking is responsible for more trouble at sea than all other things put together.

On Boat Shows

MARCH, 1913

There is no doubt but that all the real boaters and yachters have lost interest in these annual exhibitions we call shows. I know thousands of yachtsmen, but neither at the Boston nor New York show were there many of them present. The majority of the people were outsiders, sightseers, the same crowd you see at chicken, dog, horse, candy, or cement shows. These people parade around, gawk at the boats and engines, collect circulars, and go—but leave no money behind. A few years ago these shows were crowded with real people who looked, listened, and bought. Why is it these shows no longer attract the yachtsmen? Novelty has worn off—perhaps. But the real reason is that with a few exceptions there is nothing exhibited that interests the real dyed-in-the-wool boatman. In the New York show there were a number of boats, beautiful pieces of work, mahogany and brass galore, but such boats do not interest a yachtsman. The only people who buy fancy craft are greenhorns or people who have money enough to keep a couple of men to scrub and dust. If instead of exhibiting these beautiful specimens of polish and metal, the builders would show some well-built, plain-finished craft, such as an experienced man will buy and use, they would get the buying crowd back again. At the New York show, with a few exceptions, the boats were craft only suitable for use on a small lake or some place where they could be kept in a boathouse and tenderly nursed. Among the few rough knock-around boats were what is called a Sea Bright Dory, and these sold like hot cakes. If you want business, show boats that the ninety-nine can and will buy, not freaks and fancy craft that only one man in a hundred wants.

On New York City Tugs

DECEMBER, 1909

A small yacht started out of an inlet on the south side of Long Island with the owner and two men on board, and disappeared. What condition she was in I do not know, but as her course lay close along the shore, and as she had only a few miles to cover, it is unlikely that she was lost through stress of weather. The probable cause of her disappearance is that she was run down and sunk by a tow of scows, as the water over which she must have voyaged is alive with those menaces to navigation. These scows mostly belong to the city of New York; no other city would employ such an antiquated and wasteful means of getting rid of its refuse. They are towed by a tug using a long hawser, and the tug has little or no control over them. When on a clear course, the tugboat men frequently set the wheel and lie down for a nap, as they know that any vessel big enough to hurt them will give these tows a wide berth. Several launches have been run down by these scow tows, and the tug has gone on never knowing that her scows had struck anything. There is one rule I would advise yachtsmen to strictly observe: Never cross close astern of a tug at night until you are positive she has no tow.

The Joy of a
Gale Aboard *Bird*

OCTOBER, 1911

Despite booming cannons, shrieking whistles, and cheering crowds, Rudder *reported that when* Sea Bird *left the Rhode Island Yacht Club in June of 1911, "the air seemed charged with . . . gloom and foreboding." To many observers, the 25-foot yawl seemed too small to make the transatlantic passage safely. But the* Rudder *report added that the three men aboard, Tom Day, Fred B. Thurber, and T. R. Goodwin, appeared "vastly pleased with the prospect of fighting the curious storms of the Atlantic in a boat hardly large enough to turn about in."*

I am going to ask you to leave home for an hour or so and join me on *Sea Bird*. The time I want you is, say, between one o'clock and two o'clock on the afternoon of June 22nd. You can sit on the house or stand in the companion, whichever place you prefer. At first, finding yourself suddenly off the land and nearly halfway across the Atlantic, with a strong breeze blowing and a high sea running, you would be a bit frightened; but after a few minutes, realizing that there was no danger, you would settle down to enjoy the experience of running a gale in a small boat.

Looking around on every side you would see huge seas racing away from southwest to northeast, great hill-like masses of intensely blue water, with their heads crowned with crests of breaking, frothing white, that as they swept past seethed and hissed like a nest of angry serpents. These blue heaps, foam-capped, extend from horizon to horizon, rolling, running, leaping, seeming at times to play together like young dogs, and then again to spring at each other like angry tigers, tearing and frothing as they roll over and over in a mass of white and blue. In the center of this turmoil is *Sea Bird*, the only thing except sea and sky within radius of sight, a speck of wood, lifting aloft a pair of swinging, reeling spars and one strip of wind-rounded sail. Watch her! She lurches to the top, pauses for an instant, cradled in the broken crest, and then with a rush of wind and a cloud of spray dashes down the steep side into the trough. Here becalmed for an instant she seemingly hesitates, gives a lee-lurch and weather-roll, and then up again and over.

Two men are on her deck, one at the tiller, alert, active; the other, quietly seated on the weather side, his body close down in the pit and his arm over the combing, holds an oil can. He keeps a sharp lookout astern over his shoulder, as does the helmsman.

"Big one!" he exclaims, and from the can's spout lets fall a drop or two of oil.

The helmsman measures the breaker with his eye, and at the right instant gives *Bird* a touch of the helm. The broken, seething mass rushes for the stern, its feet strike the oil, slip up, and it falls and slides past in a hissing foam-patch on either side.

"That was a corker," says the man at the helm.

"Good old *Bird*!" exclaims his mate, giving the little boat an affectionate pat.

So she runs, making 5 to 6 knots over seas from 15 to 20 feet from trough to crest. At first a bit fearful, you soon grow to love this racing with the gale; all thought of danger vanishes from the mind and you make yourself a part of the plucky little boat, and laugh and sing as she leaps and swings over the crests.

But the long hours of this constant watching and racing bring a strain on muscles and mind, and the ocean under the lash of the increasing wind is beginning to get ugly. The seas crush and tumble together, break and drop over, and even in the trough the water is ragged and full of swirls.

It is beginning to tell on *Bird*; she has lost some of her jaunty confidence, and slips and staggers a bit as if tired. It is time for boat and man to have a rest.

I go below and have a look at the glass; still falling, more wind to come and more sea; better lay-to now before it gets worse. Having made up your mind to lay-to, the next thing is to decide what under. If it's not blowing too hard, I usually lay-to with *Bird* or any yawl under a close-reefed mainsail, but in a stiff gale this is too much cloth. A small jib and a reefed jigger is sometimes good sail, but no rule can be laid down; it depends on the boat, the sea, and the heft of the wind. I decided to try *Bird* under a reefed jigger, and if not enough to add the mizzen staysail.

Taking the helm I called all hands: "Set the jigger and stand by to take off the jib"; and round comes *Bird* on a port helm, and as the headsail drags, slatting and rattling down the stay, she pokes her nose into the wind's eye, and then falling off, rides the next big one half-breast to, like a wing-tired gull.

We watched her for a minute or two and then, seeing the jigger was not enough, gave her the mizzen staysail. Better; but perhaps after all she will ride easier and more comfortably to the sea-anchor. Then she will lie head to it; so we rig the anchor.

Several years ago I met Captain Andrews, the man who crossed the Atlantic in a small craft called *Dark Secret*, and in our conversation asked what he used for a sea-anchor or drogue. He told me he used his anchor, just letting it go with all the rode, and that it held the boat's head up. I tried the same plan and found it to work well, as long as the sea heads were not running, but at such a time there was not sufficient resistance and the boat was apt to be thrown and brought beam-to. To prevent this I added a board to the anchor, lashed across the arms and flukes. This makes an excellent drogue and does not take up any room, the anchor being there anyway and the board stowing in a small space. A drogue is clumsy, and takes up a lot of room.

After lying-to for a few minutes, we rigged the anchor, bent on about 300 feet of rode, and let it go. It tailed out ahead as *Bird* was traveling stern-first at the rate of two knots or more, and when it came to rest it was floating about two seas off and I suppose ten fathoms below the surface. It did its duty, and with her nose pointed right into the wind the little yawl rode with an easy motion and dry decks.

As soon as she was anchored, and the rode well-armed with old canvas, I jumped below for a dry and a rest, and the boys soon followed. In the cabin out of the rush of the wind, and the boat riding with an easy, sweeping motion, you would hardly have known that you were at sea. I have been lots more uncomfortable anchored in a harbor.

"What would the crepe-wavers think of this? A forty-mile breeze and a big sea, and all hands down below taking things easy," says the mate.

"I suppose they picture us wailing and praying, clinging in white-faced agony to the mast while the merciless ocean dashes its rude billows over our half-numbed bodies," says the skipper. "Ain't it awful, this here ocean. My! What would mother say."

Let's take a peep into the cabin that afternoon about three o'clock and see what the terror-stricken mariners are doing. The skipper is half-lying, half-sitting forward, chocked in between the bunks, needle and palm in hand, leisurely sewing the seams of a bag to hold the colors; the engineer is writing up his log, and the mate is stewing a dish of prunes; outside *Bird* and the gale are having things all to themselves.

At this same hour not fifty leagues away in the same latitude a large passenger steamer has slowed down in order to quiet the nerves and stomachs of her passengers. I met one of these passengers afterwards and he described that day of storm as one of untold misery. Verily do men view gales of wind through their stomachs.

Once in a while we would take a look outside. "Don't worry," *Bird* seemed to say, "I am on this job." And she was, God bless her, making beautiful weather of it.

After stewing the prunes the mate got restive and, clothed only in a shirt, wandered up and down the deck. In one of his perambulations he discovered a big shark alongside. Mr. Shark leisurely swam around the boat, keeping an eye cocked on the deck, hoping something eatable might come his way. It did. Thurber coaxed him up with a piece of pork and then with a pistol plugged a few lead pellets into his carcass. Looking very much disgusted, Mr. Shark swam sadly off, but after that there was no more bathing.

The wind held all that afternoon, and by night it was still blowing hard. We hung a light in the mizzen rigging, and leaving one man on watch, turned in for a sleep. The hand on watch sat inside by the companion and did his best to keep awake by being as uncomfortable as possible, which was easy. I fell asleep and was waked up by being pitched head-on into a mess of pans and kettles. The next morning it was still blowing and a big sea running. We spent the time clearing up below and getting our clothes dried out. At noon I got a bad sight, and at 2 p.m., it having let up some, we set the jib and bore away on our course. From the indifferent sights I had, we made her drift 77 miles in 24 hours; as this was very nearly in the right direction, the result was received with cheers.

That evening, a dirty, mean, dying sea made things unpleasant, as the wind had gone and *Bird* was tossed and rolled about like a football in a barrel. We came to anchor again, but she lay in the trough and gave us a most unhappy night. It was the worst of the voyage. Sleep was impossible. Outside it poured rain, and inside everything was damp and miserable. Our fuel was down to one tank, and this we were anxious to save in case we got a headwind or dead calm. At daylight we hove in the anchor, set the jib, and ran off, in the midst of a terrific squall, which happily proved to be our last—a fierce farewell to the Gulf Stream. I never saw such lightning, and if there is anything I am afraid of, it is lightning. It flashed overhead and on all sides, and the wind blew in wild gusts, churning up the dying sea, and dashing spray, hail, and rain at us in clouds. It was a wild morning, but at about ten o'clock things began to improve, and at noon under a bright blue sky with all sail set, *Bird* was flying to the east at a speed of four or better. But I was all in; the last three days had taken the vim out of my bones and muscles, and I was stranded high but not dry below. The boys kindly took my watch that night, and after a good sleep I came out as fresh as ever.

In a voyage of this kind there is and always must be a certain amount of anxiety carried by the man in command. The success of the venture depends to an extent upon his skill and judgment, and he is constantly under a mental strain. I know and have felt the difference between being captain or crew, or being captain or passenger. If another man is in command, I can go below at night, turn in, and sleep like an infant, but if in command, no matter how fine the weather and clean the navigation, there is always hanging over your mind a cloud of responsibility that follows you night and day on deck and below. You cannot take if off with your hat and put it on again with your oiler. The skipper's happiest time is when he has three miles of water under his vessel's keel, a clean sky overhead, and no ships around; then he can go to bed and turn off a fine length of sleep. Happy was I when we were once clear of land and out of the track of the shipping, and my worries were cut down to fear of the wind going ahead or one of the crew falling overside.

The one great danger of boating in shallow or deep water is falling overboard. This is a menace that is always present, and at night and in bad weather nine times out of ten it would be fatal. Even if the accident happened under the helmsman's eye, it would be doubtful if he could get around quick enough to cover the spot or come within hailing distance of the man in the water. We were constantly on guard against this, and I never let the boys get on the main-boom until I saw personally that the sheet was properly belayed and the jam hitched. This is a trap that has thrown many a man to his death. Whenever they were reefing or lowering sail or working forward, if at the helm, I always eased her down, so that if a man went, we could get him. We had lifelines rove, and in bad weather body lashings. *Bird*'s boom cocks up, so the danger of being struck by that was small, but several times I was thrown off my feet by lurchers, and they had to be constantly guarded against.

Lurchers are seas that run at right angles to the true sea, and strike a vessel on the beam or quarter. They are wholly lawless and cannot be guarded against, being outcasts who, driven to desperation, are rushing frantically about seeking a place to live. I made a special study of these vagabonds and came to the conclusion that they are the result of what geologists call a squeeze. Two large seas running with the wind come together, end to end, and the force squeezes out a portion of the ends; this rises to the top and rushes along the crest, seeking to regain its level by dropping into a cleft or trough. It is these lurchers that do the damage to steam vessels, as they hit them on the bow or quarter, and leaping up pyramid-shape topple over on board. They would hit *Bird* on the beam or quarter and heave her over until her deck was under, and then letting go, she would right with a fierce weather jerk. There was no warning, and you had always to be on guard against them, if any sea was running astern.

Now let's see what the log says on June 23d:

> *"This day begins with S.W. wind and moderate sea. At 3 a.m. bore away; at 4 a.m. heavy squalls; running under jib and jigger. At 8 a.m. clearing; sights at 8:14. Clear to 10*

a.m. Fine weather rest of day with strong S. by W. wind and moderate sea. Fine night. Position at noon: 40° 30' North, 45° 02' West."

That entry marks the end of our bad weather and the beginning of our good. From then on until we came on the Portuguese coast we had fine days and fine nights.

By June 25th, the wind had increased and gone to east of south. A clear sky, except for a belt of fine weather clouds, and a moderate sea. At 1 a.m. reefed mainsail, at 9 a.m. shook out reefs; at noon the run was 117 miles, not bad as the wind was forward of the beam, and no current. That day at 10 a.m. we ran into a patch of green water. Thurber and I noticed it at the same time and called out together, "Shoal water." It is unquestionably a shoal, but when we say shoal we mean an ocean shoal, a patch of rock, a mountaintop with probably 100 to 200 fathoms on it. It was about half-a-mile wide and approximately in 40° latitude and 40° 02' longitude. To the east of it some 50 miles, a rock was reported sighted some years ago, and is marked on the chart with a question mark after it. There are numbers of these vigias in this part of the ocean, but they are no longer marked on the chart. I don't question that in the vicinity of the Azores there are several peaks that do not come near enough to the top to show, and it is unreasonable to assert that these vigias never existed because they do not exist now. I know shoal water when I see it, and when a boat sails suddenly out of deep blue into a green patch and crosses and leaves that green patch again just as suddenly, it is bottom and nothing else.

But numbers of ships have passed there, and why did they not report it? Because they don't see it—or if they do, put it down to cold water. You see hundreds of things in little vessels you never notice in large ones. In a small craft your eye is close to the water, and your gaze is constantly on it. In a large vessel you are 10 to 50 feet from the water, and your eye dwells on the sea at a distance and not close alongside; you watch the surface at an angle and not at a perpendicular.

In a large vessel a man is on the sea, but in a small one he is with the sea. The aim of the owners of a passenger steamer is to surround the voyager with objects that will cause him to forget that he is at sea; they create as much as possible a land environment. He is roofed over and barricaded in so that he cannot see the sky overhead or the sea beneath except by craning his neck over the rail. The ship is made as nearly as possible to resemble a hotel, and the foremost boast of the owners is that she resembles a land tavern. In a few years they will do away with what little deck is left, and the passengers will voyage to Europe completely under cover, the only view they have of the ocean being through stained glass port-lights.

What can such cooped beings know of the sea? Of its beauty, its grandeur, its loneliness? They never see it as we do, sleeping under the stars, or laughing and romping under the sun. Have they joined it and the moon in a watch, when wind and wave are dancing the dance of silver? The *Bird*, the sea, and I had many a watch together. Let us spend another wild, windy four hours, say the night of June 26th or the early morning of June 27th.

The wind is south by east and the course east, so that it is a point forward of the beam. *Bird* is under close-reefed main and jib and jigger, and is making 5 knots, hour in and hour out. If you have ever driven a small boat at a continual 5-knot gait with a strong beam wind, through a heavy beam sea, you can take what I am going to tell you and warp it into a picture.

The next man is sleeping or trying to sleep, chocked in between the bunks, when the cry comes down the hatch, "One bell." He sits up, yawns, stretches, and sings back, "All right." He knows the boat is going, for he can hear the gurgle of the water under the chines, and feel the speed tremble, and if that is not evidence enough of what is doing outside, every ten seconds she hits a hole and drops into it with a crash, or takes a smasher under the quarter that shakes up the kitchen and sets the pots and pans a-ringing. A grope for the electric light switch and a small glim is turned on, which gives light sufficient to find your clothes, a drink, and a Uneeda or two. This hearty meal done, and it is on oilers; this is performed with your head poked out of the companion. It is black as pitch, the sky is ink to you coming out of the light, and the ocean a mass of whiteheads, the helmsman shining like a man armor-clothed in the binnacle rays, his oilers dripping, the jigger a swollen shadow, and the wind whistling and woofing.

"How's she doing?"

"Fine. Had her up to southeast by south nearly all the watch; she's just broke off again to southeast. Pretty wet. Sea's more ahead and breaking nasty."

"What'd you make?"

"A good twenty! Any sleep below?"

"Not much. She pounds like the devil. I wish we could let her off a point or two or this darn wind would haul to the west'ard! All right, I'll take her now."

The weary one crawls below and helmsman and *Bird* are left together for a four-hour tussle with wind and sea.

It is eye-wearying, watching the compass; the light is unsteady, and the glass frosty with salt. The stars are out, and the helmsman gets *Bird* on the course and picks out the largest one he can find ahead; keeping the dancing point of light 'twixt weather shroud and mast, he steers the course with an occasional glance at the card to make sure he is holding her true. It is wet work, and if she wasn't making her course, you would be anything but contented. Five knots and due east makes up for a lot of discomfort, and you whistle and sing as she drives into it and flings the sea in handfuls at you. The sea is tall and rugged. Not a sea that would bother you if you had it over your shoulder, but swinging in on the rigging it is somewhat nasty. Off the wind, *Bird* would carry all the rags, but sometimes even the reefed mainsail seems too much.

The watch below are hugging themselves that that mainsail is tied in, for it means no call, and five wet, cold minutes on deck. At first when called out we came with our clothes on, but a few experiences taught us to leave what dry things we had below, and it was a funny sight reefing in a squall, the rain and hail pouring down on the unprotected hides of the crew, as they jumped about the cabin top. Reef and run, was the word.

I always hated to call the boys out, and for this reason usually reefed before the other man went below. It does not pay to carry sail after a certain point; it simply means discomfort without adequate gain. This is especially the case if there is a sea running.

This belt of south wind extended from 45° to 33°, and we were about six days in crossing it. It began with a good whole-sail breeze and gradually increased, being strongest between 40° and 37° when we made a run of 123 miles in 24 hours. The maximum strength was 30 miles, and like a trade it had its periods, being strongest at noon and midnight. It usually began at sunrise from a little east of south, and following the sun had swung to west of south by four o'clock. The sky was clear except for a belt of clouds, often completely enclosing the horizon, and the air warm but not oppressive as we had it farther along. It was perfect ocean weather, and could we have had the wind aft, those days would have been some of the most pleasant of our passage. Instead they were the most disagreeable and tiresome. It was impossible to remain on deck, unless clothed in oilers, as *Bird* threw water like a young fire engine, so we had to pass the hours of watch below. All we had to read was one novel, a copy of *Life*, and the ads in the back of Brown's Almanac. I was teaching the boys to navigate, and this helped kill some hours. We had one good coat, an Impervo made by Armstrong, and all hands wore that. It never leaked a drop, and came through the passage in fine condition. The oilers gave out at the knees and elbows, the constant rubbing making them leak.

I started to take a four-hour watch with you, but have run completely off the course; but while we have been talking the dawn has appeared, a faint glow in the northeast, and the wind is letting go, as it does with the coming of the sun.

I love the dawn, and that is why my choice of watches is the middle. The dawn is the coming of life, the springing into existence of youth, laughter, gladness, all that is inspiring and delighting. The heart rushes ahead to greet it; the eye dances with eagerness to catch the increasing light; you shout as you would at an advancing army whose suddenly discovered banners give promise of rescue and victory. Oh, for a trumpet blast or a roll of drums—for look, see the King is coming. Red, serene, he lifts his head, a single black belt of clouds across his brow; then he rolls proudly up, pouring out like a flood of wine a stream of crimson that lanes the sea from horizon to horizon. The clouds doff their colors, slip back, melt, and pass away, and he begins his daily swing, majestic, unattended, the lord master and arbitrator of all.

After I had taken the old gentleman's bearing by the standard compass, I bowed with great deference, for he was the very person we needed, as our first landfall was getting close aboard. At quarter to eight we hove *Bird* to, so as to get sights, to eat, and to clean up below and about the decks. The sight put her in 35° 25′, and the islands are in 31°. But we had worked considerably to north, and were in 40° 21′ that day at noon. No getting down if it held, but at noon it dropped off, and gave us our chance; putting her under power we headed to the southward. All afternoon the sea kept going, and by night it was smooth and the wind just a whisper.

June 28th and at noon we are out seventeen days from Wasque Point and eighteen days from Providence, and the nearest of the Azores how far away? The log reads:

"This day begins with cloudless sky, light S. by E. wind and smooth sea. Under power until 5 a.m. Fine day: finest of all. Good sights. At noon Corvo bore E. by S. ¾ S., distant 103 miles. Under power again at quarter to one p.m. Calm all afternoon and night. At 12:30 a.m. light off starboard bow. Steamer."

We had 33 miles of latitude and 97 miles of longitude, and I told the boys to look out for land about five o'clock, right ahead, with Corvo on the port bow and Flores on the starboard. At midnight a steamer passed some five miles away, headed east. Our usual luck. Every steamer we passed went by in the night.

At four o'clock, Thurber took the helm and I went below. It was a calm, misty morning, and at that time you could not see far. A few minutes after five I heard the deck hailing.

"Hi, Skipper, land ahead."

"How does it bear?"

"Right ahead. Looks like two big rocks, one on the port bow and one on the starboard. We are aimed to go right between them."

"Corvo and Flores. Keep her on the same course"; and turning over I went to sleep again.

Thus did *Bird* make the Azores, at 5 a.m. the 29th day of June, being out 17 days, 16 hours, and 30 minutes.

Dry Days
on *Detroit*

DECEMBER, 1912, and JANUARY, 1913

Day set out again across the Atlantic in the summer of 1912. The 35-foot double-ended Detroit *looked like "an overloaded decked-in lifeboat," according to a* Rudder *report, but Day had high ambitions for the little powerboat: to skipper her from Detroit, Michigan, to St. Petersburg, Russia—a 6,000-mile voyage. The first leg, from Detroit to New York, took about ten days. Then Day and crewmen Walter H. Moreton, Charles C. Earle, and an unidentified "paid hand" went to sea. The crossing to Ireland was difficult. Two days out, the crew discovered the water supply was oily. Four days out, the boat began showing a tendency to list. The paid hand became intimidated by a storm and, Day reported, "lay down and skulked the rest of the passage."*

This excerpt picks up Day's account two weeks after Detroit *had left Martha's Vineyard.*

Tuesday, July 30th, it blew hard from the southwest, and by 5 a.m. a nasty sea had picked up, *Detroit* steered wildly, and no slowing-down seemed to do any good; she would take the bit and run a sea, not the slightest feeling to the helm. In fact, for all the good it was for those minutes, the rudder might just as well have been left ashore. Then she would start to broach, and it took some helming to recover control in time to stop her getting the best of the game. An hour or so of this fun made my shoulders and arms ache, and after she had shipped a couple of combers that nearly knocked my legs from under me, I stopped the engine and let her lie to. The lady quietly dropped into the trough, turned her stern slightly up to the run of the sea, and lay there as comfortable as a kid in a cradle. This was the largest sea we had during the passage, but it was nothing extraordinary and would have looked small beside the one we rode in *Sea Bird*. I measured the taller waves, and should judge that from trough to crest they were between 10 and 12 feet, but they were steep and not as good for riding as a large and longer sea.

Moreton and I overhauled the provision locker hunting for canned fruit, and luckily found two cans which we hid away, as we thought somebody might be ill and need it. At this time we were suffering severely from thirst, the canned fruit having given out and leaving nothing but soup and vegetables out of which to get some fluid. I tried over and over again to catch some rainwater, but only succeeded once in getting a real drink. Talk about your wines and your nectars—not for all the vintage of Champagne and Burgundy would I have parted with that half-cup of rain. The trouble was everything was crusted with salt, and it never rained hard enough to wash this salt off so that any rain dripping from sail or spars or deck was brackish and undrinkable. If you held a cup out to catch the drops it was sure to waylay as much spray as it did rain. We used to stand at the wheel with our tongues out catching the raindrops, but they burned rather than cooled our parched mouths. Every drop of water wasted during my life, every spring, brook, and well that I had drank at came to my memory, and there were hours when you could have had my clothes and all that the pockets held for a thimbleful of clean drinkable water. I had a dollar bill in my pants pocket which I took out frequently and showed to my watchmate, while we discussed sadly the utter worthlessness of money. Money—what is money? Out on the ocean far from succor on a sinking ship, men have for the first time realized what it is. Men starving, dying of thirst, gold in plenty around them can tell you what money is. How sorrowfully we contemplated that dirty dollar bill, and what contempt we had for it, miserable thing it was, powerless to obtain even a glass of water. Several times during the day I started and tried to run her off, but she cut up, and we were obliged to bring to again. I was afraid she might broach and ship a sea, and one of us go overboard, or be thrown and break a leg or arm, so chose the safer plan of lying still. At 3 p.m. the glass started to rise, but the wind still kept blowing and the sea running.

At 10 p.m., the wind having let go and the sea dropped, we were once more under way and standing the course. The sky began clearing up, the moon came out, the sea went down, and we made good time. Wednesday, the 31st, turned out to be one of our few good days, so far as overhead was concerned. At eight o'clock I had a sight, and found to our joy that we were twenty miles ahead of the reckoning, and about nine hundred miles from Queenstown. The error arose through not allowing enough for drift when we hove to in the sou'wester, but as it was on the right side of the balance, nobody kicked. The latitude at noon was out three miles, not bad for five days' reckoning.

By this time, the work and strain of the voyage were beginning to tell, and one bad night at a time was about all we cared to stand. Loss of sleep is the worst of all; hunger, thirst, and constant holding on you can suffer and laugh at, but when you cannot sleep you get nerve tired and broken. I had been sparing the boys as much as possible, but about this time I realized that if my feet were to stay under me I must spare myself, and so began nursing my strength to make it last out the passage.

The main thing in preserving your vigor during such a trip as this is to lie down flat on your back as often and as long as possible. Stonewall Jackson, whose soldiers' legs won for him the majority of his battles, when he halted his men on the march always insisted on their lying flat to rest, and it is unquestionably the best way to rest the body and limbs, especially the spine. It is tiring of the spine that weakens your resistance to fatigue. When we could no longer stand the strain, we were obliged to heave-to and take a rest; a few hours lying quiet gave all hands a chance to sleep, and we woke up refreshed, and anxious and ready to go ahead again. But better than all was a day or perhaps two days of light weather; when the sea going down, the vessel was comparatively steady and we had a chance to move around on deck and to rest in peace below. If a little sunshine came with this so much the more glorious, and we could shed some of our clothes, which hung on and burdened us like armor on the backs of the crusaders. At one time I had on five shirts, waistcoat, coat, and raincoat. Even then I felt chilly. It was a relief to shed some of these slates and expose the bare rafters to the sun and warm air.

One Sunday about this period of the voyage we had a fine spell for a few hours, and Moreton and I had our first shave. The stars know we needed it. A large pail of hot water, plenty of soap, towels, and off with the clothes, and what a wash. I felt a hundred times better after that scrub and scrape. We lashed a looking glass to the mast, and after an extensive lathering of Williams' Soap, went at it. Talk about deforestation—that was some hewing down. The mate refused to join us in this battle of the tubs, and so remained bewhiskered and dirty several more days. Once cleaned up, Moreton and I felt a constituted aristocracy, and rather held aloof from the uncleaned, unshaven portion of the crew.

Dirt and whiskers are exceedingly depressing. The dirtier I get and the more whiskers my chin and cheeks exhibit, the more depression takes charge of me. The spirit of the hobo liveth not within me. For several days I determined to shave, would wake up and go on deck, my mind fully made up to flourish the razor, but something would happen and it was put off for a change of weather or a change of watch or something until at last that Sunday, driven almost to a frenzy by the itching of the hairy forests, I tackled the job and soon had it over.

What made it so disagreeable was that your face and hair were encrusted with salt, and this salt worked into the pores of the skin and burned like pepper. It was especially bad in the corners of your eyes, making them sting. The salt clung to your hair like icicles on a sheep's back, and matted it together. But all these disagreeable things were forgotten after sticking your head into a bucket of warm water and sousing around a bit. That Sunday is deeply carved in my memory as one of the happiest days of my life.

To all men who are exposed to incessant toil and privations, there come hours of depression, times when all around looks black, and obstacles ahead seemingly enlarge in dimension and appear to vastly increase their power of preventing successful progress. The imagination, losing its buoyancy, no longer floats gaily aloft but drifts and droops down, down until it hovers wing-weary over a sea of despondency. This condition is purely the result of physical strain, the resultant mental effect being produced by the stagnation and poisoning of the blood. The best antidote for this condition is conversation on topics wholly divorced from the subject nearest to your life. Talk about things miles away—picking daisies, milking cows, how to inflate balloons, why Hannibal failed to assault Rome, probable age of the moon, who discovered America, or anything in farming, science, literature, history, or art. If you have no one to talk to, sing, whistle, laugh, repeat all the poetry you know, do anything to keep your mind away from your present situation.

That we could hold no pleasant conversations was one of the main drawbacks on *Detroit*. Owing to the barking of the exhaust, except when in the fore cabin it was impossible to converse except by shouting. I kept my ears stuffed with cotton wool and in this way could hear what was said, but with open ears it was impossible to catch a word unless it was yelled. It was promised that we should have a way of silencing the exhaust, but the method provided did not work, and we tried every means of getting rid of this nuisance. The introducing of water did some to lessen the racket, but this was at times disagreeable owing to the volcanic explosions that took place, driving out lumps of salt as big as a walnut and at other times a rain of dirty water. How we used to welcome the hour when for a few minutes the engine was shut off for a look over and the hideous uproar ceased. The drumming in the stack was so bad that we added a piece of pipe and carried it above the funnel top, but this only exchanged a ringing bark for a sharp one. It is a wonder that nobody has been able to invent a thoroughly efficient muffler.

If I ever build a boat in which to go to sea, she will have an efficient muffler and an exhaust not only through the stack but another well forward. This latter will be carried through the cabin and be used to warm and keep dry that apartment. Had we had this device on *Detroit*, it would have added greatly to our comfort. How often did we bewail the waste of heat aft and wish that we had a portion of it in the fore cabin. A pipe from the exhaust carried through the fore cabin and turned on occasionally would have kept our clothing and bedding dry, and the gasses being sent adrift at the bow would have gone clear of the vessel and not bothered the man at the wheel. The only comfort to be had out of the noisy exhaust was in thick weather; it beat a fog-horn for keeping up a warning, and that was the only time we gave it our blessing.

Having come down on the Bishop Rock track on Wednesday, July 31st, the weather clearing up, we had a sight, a good one, and found our reckoning very close to being correct. About 10 a.m. we sighted a German to the south about two miles and set the ensign; he set his, and knowing he had seen and would report us we again headed the course. At noon I had the latitude and after working it up, put her about 900 miles off the Fastnet. With high hopes that the weather would be good for the rest of the voyage, we felt pretty sure of making that Rock in six days and perhaps a half-day sooner. But before going along, let me tell of our encounter with the *S. S. Amerika*.

When we first saw *Amerika*, she was off the port bow and running parallel to our course, distant about three miles. We supposed she would pass us, without altering her course, so stood on ours. About five minutes after we sighted her, she altered her course and stood right down on *Detroit*. I then ordered the helm shifted and we stood up to meet her, steering about north. While we were standing to meet her, one of the boys suggested that we try and get some bottled water, and I took the two flags, Y and R, from the binnacle locker and gave them to the mate to hoist. This was at least five minutes after we turned *Detroit*'s head towards the *Amerika*. So had she stood her course, we would not have hoisted the water signal; but as she evidently intended to speak to us, we took advantage of the situation. When she ranged alongside she reversed her propellers, stopped, and I turned *Detroit* around and went back close in under her side. But it was like shouting across Broadway and talking to a man on the roof of a six-story building with a mob of people surrounding him. About two thousand humans were lined up from stem to stern and they were all talking and shouting, waving and making snapshots.

I saw the captain come down off the upper deck with several men with pails of water, and called to him several times that we could not use pail water and wanted some in bottles. We had no place to put pail water, the tanks being foul, and it would not stay in the buckets. Instead of listening, he kept shooting questions at us. He wanted to know where we were bound. On being told, he shouted back, "Do you know you are one thousand miles from Queenstown?" As we had had good sights that day, this was news. He then kept yelling to come alongside. I didn't like to go close alongside; the last mix-up had made me a bit fearful of getting a knock that might start things along the upper works. From *Amerika*'s deck the water undoubtedly looked smooth, but along her side the sea was running two or three feet high. What I wanted to do was to get a heaving line from the steamer, bend on my life preservers, and send them aboard. They could lash these around a case of bottled water and heave it overside, and then we could pick it up. At last, after much shouting and being unable to make them understand, I gave it up in disgust and, putting *Detroit*'s head east again, called out, "Please report me," and left.

August 3rd.—This day begins fine with calm, bright skies. At 8 a.m. had good sights. At noon we were 480 miles from the Fastnet. Shake hands, boys, four days more and we will see either the tall tower on the surf-beaten rock or else old Mizzen Head, the gray bleak headland that Ireland thrusts out like a buttress of a fortress to shoulder and smash the surges of the boisterous Atlantic. We stopped for an hour at noon and gave the motor a thorough cleaning and overhaul, at the same time fixing up about the decks and getting our clothes aired out and the cuddy cleaned. At noon, when our watch went below, we promised the mate's watch a treat at the next eight bells. This was one of the hidden cans of fruit. Being carefully opened, it was found to contain thirteen half-pieces, and these were divided with the juice among all hands, the extra piece being given to the paid man. It was delicious, and to our parched throats the juice tasted like nectar. To try and better the water, we punched a hole in the top of the port tank and with a piece of rubber tubing drew off the fluid from the top; this was slightly better, but a mouthful was all you could get down and then only with reluctance. I chewed raisins and drank lime juice; this for a time would assuage the thirst. The eagerness for water was strongest at waking from sleep, and that was when we were forced to take a mouthful of that cocktail.

August 4th was another hurrah day. It began with a clear sky and a grand good westerly wind, and we were going full speed and covering distance. At noon she had 156 miles to her credit. Things were cheerful fore-and-aft. If this only lasts, boys, Monday night for a landfall. The good weather kept up all that afternoon and night. The usual overhauling of clothes and other belongings took place. What was not wanted was thrown overboard, and a general cleaning up was under way. By this time *Detroit* looked rather forlorn and bedraggled. She had had a terrific washing, being constantly driven into it. The paint was gone off her topsides, her deck and fittings were salted and bleached, her funnel was coated with white rime, and she was foul with dirt. It was impossible to do anything to keep her clean, as it was only at rare intervals she would hold still long enough to allow you to wield a mop or broom, and then we were usually too tired to tackle what was not absolutely necessary work.

Early in the voyage she rolled the mop overboard. Luckily I saw it go and put back after it. It took some jockeying to get the darn thing, but at last somebody grasped the four inches of handle sticking out and hauled it aboard. In the sou'wester of July 30th, the steering wheel, which had shown signs of weakness, began to go to pieces and I bethought of the mop handle. This we sawed up, and with it we fished the wheel so that it was stronger than ever and lasted until we made port.

When the boat was laid out, it was decided by the owner and builder that as she was a western boat everything on and in her possible should be of western make. Only one or two things were from the east; one of these was the steering wheel. It was a cast brass affair and soon went to pieces. Brass wheels are no good; either use iron or, better still, a good wooden wheel. This steering wheel was the only thing on the boat that broke or fell down, which is a braw card for the builder.

That Sunday was the best day we had east of the Banks, and the boat made the fastest time of the passage. For several hours she logged 6.8 knots. If this weather only keeps up, we'll save our guess, we said at noon, when the position was dotted down on the chart. August 5th came in like a young colt—clear sky, brisk northerly wind, but not enough to kick up a bothersome sea. At noon we stopped for thirty minutes to get a sight and overlook the motor. The sight worked up put us 179 miles from Fastnet, which bore N. 70° E. One more day's run like the last and we would see Ireland at Tuesday noon or perhaps two hours earlier. But alas, it was not to be. At 2 p.m. the wind backed into the N.N.W. and began to blow; by night it was very close to being a gale, and a steep sea was running. Our fighting blood was up. Go she must, wind or no wind, sea or no sea, and that night we drove *Detroit* as she had never been driven before. That was the one night I would have liked to have had you there. Then you would have seen and realized what a small boat can do.

During the two good days we had managed to get her pumped nearly dry, and to right *Detroit* up so she stood fairly straight on her feet, but the heavy weather brought a quick return of our troubles. She took a worse list than ever, getting over with the wind's help so that in the lee lurches she put the starboard rail clean under and the reflux of the heave broke into her midships in buckets and sometimes barrelfuls. I don't like lee water. Weather water you expect; but when it begins to heave in over the lee rail, it gets frosty. We had the boat cover lashed along the weather side to keep the spray off, and now and again a sea would hit this with a whack and fly up, throwing a mass of spume clear across her like a burst of rain. I was obliged to stow the trysail as it was helping to increase the heel. We had the weather tank filled and all the deck lead piled on the windward side, but despite all this she was gradually increasing the list and getting more and more loggy. That was the worst night of the trip, and I never turned in or was off my feet while dark lasted.

At nine o'clock the engineer reported the batteries running low, so we stopped and ran the engine to charge up. Before stopping, I put her head west, so bringing her starboard side to the wind, to let the sea roll the ballast back again. While lying-to, we fought the water down with the engine pump and deck pump and got her nearly dry fore-and-aft, but the midships compartment had a foot or two swashing around.

At 11:30 we were under way again. The wind was blowing hard at times, squalls filled with fine rain. This was the heaviest breeze we had crossing. At times it may have gotten up to Force 7, or what sailors call a moderate or half-gale—that is, a wind velocity of 35 to 40 miles. Of course a northerly wind with this velocity is heavier than a southerly wind of the same velocity, being colder, and a sea kicked up by a northerly wind is always worse for a small boat than one coming from a southern quadrant. A sea from the south has more run to it, whereas a north sea is tall and sharp. Altogether, that night was what we call a dirty night, but still it had its compensations.

Take all the sports of the world that depend for their incitement upon forward movement, and there is none that can compare with running a small boat in a heavy seaway. A sailing craft offers more excitement than a power vessel, but even *Detroit* could warm your blood up. As my watchmate said that night, a few hours of this glorious game was worth all we had gone through. When she made those grand rushes, descending with a smother of spray into the hollows, then seeming to slightly pause, quiver and roll, and then spring like a frightened stag up the slope, to hang for a moment on the white, bursting, hissing crest, ere she made another forward rush.

All about, ahead, astern, to weather, and alee, seemingly leaping out of the wall of darkness circling the vessel a score of fathoms distant, were masses of snow, the wind-torn heads of the surges. On one side they rushed towards you; on the other, hissing and frothing, they charged away into the blackness. Splashing and hammering of the bows, the shot-like pelting of the squall-driven spray on the weather cloth, the roaring, wailing of the wind, and the ringing in of the tireless motor, were all joined to make up our battle picture.

Heaving and rolling, we clung to the wheel or rail and shouted to drive her. Time and time again I shook my fist at the wind and cursed it, for had it held off we would have made the landfall inside of twenty-one days.

August 6th broke gloomy, with the wind chasing us as strongly as ever and the sea leaping and striking at the quarter. The clouds hung low, but it was clear enough to see the horizon and at one time it even broke so I managed to get an indifferent shot at the sun, which worked up put us within easy reaching distance of land, and I announced that keeping going we would have the Emerald Isle close aboard at eight the next morning.

Late that afternoon my strength began to give out, and at five o'clock I was putting up a desperate fight to keep on my feet; at last, realizing it was a losing battle, I called the boys and told them I would have to go below and turn in. They answered, "All right, go on. We will run her tonight, taking two-hour tricks." So I went below and turned in all standing.

If ever you voyage with the skipper of *Detroit*, you can tell what the weather is going to be for the next four hours by his actions when turning in. If he goes below with a cheery warning to keep a good lookout, offs with his oiler, hat, boots, and undercoat, you can be sure of the same or better weather; if he keeps on his boots, look out for a possible change; but if he turns in all standing, you may be sure that worse is coming. But this night I was too tired, too utterly worn out to care what the weather was going to be; blow high or blow low, I must sleep. My coat and hat came off, but I could not manage the boots, so I took 'em to bed with me. Let the ship sink—what was it to me?

I shall never forget that night. Waking up at about half-past eight and looking over on the other bunk, I was astonished to see the paid hand peacefully dozing off wrapped up in the blankets. It was his watch in the engine room. This was too much for even my tired spirit, and I went for him red-hot. Before I could grasp the hatchet, he was out of the door, across the deck, and down in the engine room. His agility was all that prevented murder on the high seas. His excuse for turning in was that Moreton and Earle did not want him to be the first to sight land, and therefore had sent him below to sleep in all night. How can a man skulk and shirk his duties when those with him are burdened and wearied almost to dropping? That night, although I knew it was impossible to do otherwise, it shamed me to desert the deck and leave the two boys to drive the ship. Reason told me that I must recruit my strength, for the next day we might make the coast in thick weather, and then the skipper would be needed at his post every minute. Thankful that we were miles from the coast, I lay down, not forgetting what a night it would have been had we been jammed down on a lee shore instead of having good water between us and the land.

A spell or so and I would awaken and in a drowsy way try to understand what was going on on deck. Now and again a sea would break over the weather side and with a crash go flying across the deck. One of these, the biggest we shipped during the passage, hit Moreton and knocked the wind out of him. Luckily he was lashed to the wheel or he might have been swept overside. The foot of my berth was in line with the door of the cuddy and, it being darker inside than out, the opening appeared a glimmering square. I would watch her roll and, as long as she came back to the vertical, turn over and go to sleep again. There was no more weather rolling; she was listed too much to starboard for that amusement.

At six I woke to find the daylight, and refreshed by my long lay in, went on deck, to find Moreton at the wheel nearly dead from want of sleep and stiff from his continued labors, he having had the trick since midnight. I sent him below at once, called the mate, who was sleeping in the engine room berth, and went to work to clean up the decks as they were in a pretty mess. As soon as I came on deck I knew by the run of the sea that *Detroit* was under the land, and looking north thought the peak of Mizzen Head showed over the thick to windward. But my eyes are not over good, so I did not say anything, the glasses being no help owing to light rain. Determining to stand on until eight before turning her head north, we kept the course. At 7:30, ship's time, the clouds broke away and I got a quick shot at the sun. The mate working this up put us about five miles east of the Fastnet. That agreeing very closely with the reckoning carried in my head through the night, we put *Detroit*'s bow north by east and stood up looking for the shore.

Standing forward searching through the glasses, at 8:13, ship's time, I saw the land plainly, the height called Hungry Hill showing distinctly above the mist. "There's the land," I said, pointing to it. For all the excitement this announcement raised, I might just as well have said, "There's the sun." The mate looked indifferently in the direction and said he saw it. Then somebody told Moreton, who was below, that the land was in sight. He simply acknowledged the information with a commonplace remark and turned over and went to sleep.

We ran close under the Seven Heads so we could see into the great cavern on its east side, the mouth being alive with thousands of shrieking gulls. At five o'clock we passed close to the Old Head of Kinsale

(Ireland) and hoisted the signal "Please report me all well." The station promptly answered, and with a heavy northwest squall helping *Detroit* along, we headed for Daunt's Rock Light Vessel. With motor, wind, and tide all in her favor, the little vessel was knocking off a good 7 knots, laying over on her starboard side so that the rail cap was half the time under the briny. But devil a bit did we care—port was in sight. "Drive her," was the cry, and drove she was.

A few minutes after we passed Kinsale, the Cunarder *Caronia* came steaming up in our wake and passed close alongside, her passengers hanging over the rail and cheering us. We must have been a sight laying over and footing it, a vessel manned by a ragged, weatherbeaten crew, everything soaked and sodden. *Caronia* wirelessed in that we were coming to the Admiralty Station at Queenstown, and the people in charge sent word through the town and woke up the whole population. At seven we passed Daunt's Rock Buoy about a mile inside the light vessel and stood up for Roches Point.

The harbor of Queenstown is a noble one, very easy of entrance and furnishing an absolutely safe anchorage. In former years it was crowded with shipping, all the Horn and Hope packets putting in here for orders, but with the passing of the square-rigger it has lost most of its canvaswinged visitors. Five came in the day we did, and this was an unusual number. An old skipper told me that years ago the harbor was at times so crowded that you could scarcely find room to anchor.

It was blowing hard nor'west with frequent squalls as we passed the Rock Buoy and made for the entrance. We could see *Caronia* come to anchor off Roches Point to land her mails and some passengers, but the only other thing afloat in sight was a small sailing craft ratching about under reefed canvas. Here was a chance to pick up a pilot, and we made for the boat. Had there been daylight to make the quay I would not have bothered with a pilot, but in the night, never having been within the harbor, we knew not where to land.

Within hailing distance we saw the craft was not a pilot but one of those open fishing boats common to the South Irish Coast. They are fine-lined, excellent sailing craft, and this one was a beauty. She hailed from the celebrated fishing port of Kinsale.

"Send a man aboard to pilot us in," I sang out.

"What'll ye give?" came back the reply.

"Never mind what I'll give. Come alongside."

"All right, sorr."

"Stop her," and *Detroit* came to a standstill and the fisherman ranged up alongside dowsing her lug as she did. There were five men in her crew.

"Where ye hail from?" they asked.

"New York, America."

"From Amerikee in that one? Ah! Yez are brave boys. It won't cost yez a penny. Jump aboard an' take 'em in, Danny."

As our pilot was coming over the rail we asked for water and they handed over a jug. For days we had longed for this moment, had gloated over the event of the first drink of good clean water. Time and time I had pictured how I would seize the jug or goblet and indulge in a long and blessed draught of the delicious fluid. The warm, lingering kiss of your best girl after a separation of years was not to be in it with that drink of precious sweet water. Moreton received the jug and offered it to me.

"Go ahead yourself," said I. He took a swallow and passed it over. I took a mouthful and passed it on. The intense desire for water was entirely gone, and we handed the jug back to its owners with not over a half-pint lost out of it.

The oldest hand in the fishing boat insisted upon presenting us with some fish just captured, but we could not use them. They looked eatable, and I like fish. Leaving the Kinsaleman to follow us in, with our pilot at the wheel we ran in between the Heads and soon saw the burst of lights ahead that marked Queenstown. The old reliable down in the engine room was chugging up its highest, and *Detroit* over on her side was punching off 6 knots or better, as though like a far-traveled steed she at last scented stable and stall.

About a mile from the town, a small green power boat crowded with cheering men ranged up alongside. This was Captain O'Regan's *Jeannie* with a crowd of reporters on board. They turned and tried to keep up with us but were no match for *Detroit*. She seemed to be going as she'd never gone before. Half-a-mile nearer and in the dusk we could make out the black mass of people lining the quays. Next we could hear the cheers. "Half speed," said the pilot, and we shot around the end of the quay and stopping and reversing swung slowly up to the landing steps. Then it broke loose, cheer after cheer, four or five thousand cheering. An uproar like the breaking of the surf, only the warm thunder of a real human welcome, an Irish welcome. A dozen persons tumbled in over the rail, the newspaper men. Moreton jumped ashore, the first to land, and amidst the din, my head swinging round and round, I heard loud calls for the captain. A man stood at the foot of the steps. I reached over and we shook hands, and a silence having come, in a few kindly words he bid us in the name of the people of Queenstown a welcome to the port and to Ireland.

A New Year's Toast

DECEMBER, 1909

Well! well! The fire is nearly gone; only a flicker of flame among the gray ash, and I must weather-bit and turn in, and this is the last of the year; tomorrow's dawn will usher in another space of time. Boys, I wish you were here, moored right beside, that I might look into your faces, shake your hands, and wish you the best of life's gifts. Many an hour I pass sitting in silence before the blaze, thinking and wondering what you are doing, what you look like, and what you really think of the Old Man and his craft. What wouldn't I give to meet you all, meet you in the flesh and warmth of presence, and not as I do by cold paper and pen. But tonight you are all with me, every man of my mighty crew. I have called you about me from worldwide ports, and as we stand together, I give you from my heart this greeting: May the year 1910 bring you and yours, prosperity and happiness, work to do, and the will and strength to do it.

3

Design

The Common Sense of
Cabin Arrangement

by L. Francis Herreshoff

JULY, 1944

Thousands of Rudder *readers in the 1940s and '50s dreamed of building a boat from one of L. Francis Herreshoff's designs in the magazine. Hundreds bought full plans, marked by clean, flowing lines, free of unnecessary quirk or embellishment. Years after his death in December, 1972, his plans continue to outsell those of any other designer.*

"He was a wisp of a man," wrote Rudder *editor Martin Luray after meeting Herreshoff a few months before his death, "almost elf-like with his moustache and goatee." Yet he was a giant among designers, with creations such as* Ticonderoga, *a racing ketch with an impressive*

win record spanning four decades; the H-28, *a 28-foot cruising ketch and* Rozinante, *a 28-foot double-ended yawl.*

This excerpt from his Rudder *series, called "The Common Sense of Yacht Design," shows he was also a literate advocate for the simple artistry reflected in his designs.*

You might think at first that cabins, like the sail area of a yacht, should be in proportion to the number of crew, but it is not so. I have known some elderly gentlemen who preferred to cruise quite alone. Not that they went single-handed—far from that, for, besides the private doctor, the captain, and mates down to the third power, there were at least twenty others ranging in rank from chief steward to greaser. Some of these gentlemen were not particularly fond of the water but used their yacht as an escape from the hundreds of suckers, leeches, and lice that made life on shore unbearable. But in the captain and crew of the yacht they found souls nearly as genuine as those who live by the sea. Of course these gentlemen's yachts were quite well over 200 feet, for they needed space to walk on. Some of the yachts had an electric horse in the after deckhouse, and in rainy weather the doctor would help the owner mount for a thrilling canter in this steam-heated structure. You can well imagine there was a great expanse of space below deck aft of the engine room, but this was usually filled up with numerous staterooms and boudoirs.

It so happened several years ago that I had to spend the night on one of these yachts and, because of certain happenings during the night, the occasion has always been impressed on my mind, so I will now try to relate it. I prefer not to give the name of the yacht or her owner, but she was a fine example of the skill of George Watson. She had the finest and perhaps the most elaborate interior I have ever seen, and that is partly what we are talking about. Although she had been built in the Clyde, the yacht had steamed over to Havre to have her accommodations installed, which matter had been entrusted to certain Parisian cabinetmakers, wood-carvers, and upholsterers. There is hardly space here to do its description full justice, but her dining salon was mostly in carved Spanish walnut in the Louis XV style. There was a ladies' boudoir adjoining, finished in white and gold with piano and draperies to match. The drawing room, which was in exquisite taste, was after the style of Louis XIV. Besides the owner's stateroom, there were rooms for the doctor, secretary and valet, and six guests' staterooms. The smoking room, I remember, was carved English oak with heavy silver mountings.

We dined well that night, though there were but three of us at table (not counting the doctor), and retired to the smoking room where liqueurs were served. As I had shown unusual interest in the yacht's cabinet work, when it was time to retire the owner instructed the steward to show me the other staterooms, which I now have good reason to remember because of later occurrences that night. One stateroom was entirely upholstered—walls, ceiling, and all—in tufted yellow satin. It was intended to be a soundproof room and was quite impressive looking. Another stateroom was completely executed in satinwood—bedstead, dressing table, and all—and much the most satinwood I had ever seen at one time (although much of it was undoubtedly veneer), and altogether too rich for my taste. I noticed a delightful odor in the room and, turning to the steward, I was shown the clothes locker of camphorwood and then the drawers of the dressing table whose sides and bottoms were of sandalwood. As the stateroom had been closed for some time, you can imagine the scent was quite strong.

The stateroom I was to occupy that night was perhaps the most remarkable room I have ever seen. It was paneled in ebony and inlaid with white holly slightly tinted in pale green and light brown at the edges. On the four walls which were perfectly smooth—or sheer we might say—were inlaid wreaths or garlands; in some cases they encircled the ports and the mirror. The ceiling was of white opalite which reflected the strong tones of the woodwork. When I expressed my astonishment at the room, the steward informed me he had never known it to be occupied although he had been with the yacht these sixteen years. As he said, "These sheets, sir, have never been slept in." After the steward had retired, I examined the room with unusual interest, for I had always been particularly interested in fine cabinet work, and I must say I had never seen the equal. Every seam was perfect. The dressing table was of black onyx with silver mountings and furnishings. Over the divan of black satin was a book cabinet with a dozen or so small volumes bound in white doeskin with silver tooling. They were quite the usual classics and ranged from Virgil to "Vanity Fair" but unfortunately for me were in French. After I had undressed and was entering bed I discovered the sheets were of heavy thick silk and was rather ashamed to think of the rude awakening these sixteen-year virgins were having as they were shamefully raped by my unlaundered pajamas.

I was soon propped up in bed to look over Virgil, but slowly and surely the silk sheets slid me down on my elbows. Finally in despair I switched off the light and lay on my back, watching the reflections from the water thrown up through the porthole as they danced on the ceiling. How long it was before I fell asleep I do not know, but I hate a new mattress high in the middle. Instead of resting comfortably as one might have expected, I was presently distressed by a most unpleasant dream. You know in most dreams one is never quite killed (or maybe I had better say drowned), but still remains conscious. Not so in this dream.

It seemed I had died some time ago and was carefully laid out on cold sheets in some sort of a tomb hung with wreaths and garlands. And in the dream a voice came to me from afar—only a murmur at first, and then quite audible. It seemed a very sober voice and spoke as follows quite slowly, "You will ne'er again see frames, nor deck beams, nor carlings. You will ne'er see bolt heads, nor screw heads, nor rivets—no, nor the clamp, nor the seams of the planking. No, never."

"Well," I said to myself, "I don't like the cast of this; *never* is a long time." But now in my dream a strange thing came to pass, for I saw I had been laid out (still dead of course) in the soundproof stateroom, the one of the yellow satin. And as I lay there, the voice was to be heard again quite clearly as it said, "You will ne'er again hear the ripple of the waves on the planking, nor the rain on the deck, nor the wind in the rigging. You will ne'er hear the tap on the mast of the halliards—no, never."

In my dream I saw that I was now laid out in the satinwood stateroom—the one with the scent of exotic woods—and sore was my travail by this time as I lay awaiting the voice to strip me of my last vestige. Soon it said, "You will ne'er again smell the salt sea air, nor the offshore breeze from the forest. You will ne'er smell pine wood, nor cedar, nor tar, nor the fainter smells of new cordage." And as I lay there I felt as if I had lost my last true friends. Oh, thought I, will this last forever? Is this the end? Is this the substance of death? If then I could have reached out and felt a hanging oilskin or grasped a hank of marline all might have been well again, but it was not to be so. Many things revolved in my mind, all mingled and confused, but strange to relate I kept repeating "——— those Parisian cabinetmakers."

But now in the dream the voice of another was heard. It seemed a younger and a kinder voice as it said: "Is he of an assurity dead?" Older voice: "Well, you may as well count him among the dead." Younger voice: "How has that come to be?" Older voice: "For he can no longer see, smell, or hear the true things of life, for he is surrounded by shams." Younger voice: "Yes, but are not the frames and the plating back of this screen?" Older voice: "To be sure the frames are still there (what is left of them), but they are all covered over with electric wires, rust, and corruption." Younger voice: "But is it not well to cover up some things of this life?" Older voice: "Never in cases of perfection, but where there is some blemish or defect, or the proportions are wrong, then for shame the thing is covered over, draped, or hidden. Take the columns of a temple, for instance. If their length, girth, and taper are exactly right to best do the work, all is well; but if they are ill-proportioned, no amount of foliation or decoration will enhance them. Take the legs of a maiden. If they are well-proportioned, the maid will not be backward in showing them; but in cases where they are a little oversize or there is some defect in the curves, then the kirtle is worn quite long." Younger voice: "But are not the frames and the deck beams rude members to gaze on?" Older voice: "Of an assurity, no, for they are of the true things of life. Without them the whole vessel would soon fall asunder."

And hereabouts my dream went from me, and the next thing I knew the sunlight was streaming in through the porthole and I saw that I was back in the ebony-paneled stateroom. You can be sure I lost no time in getting up, but as I was dressing the steward knocked on the door and entered. Steward speaking: "My word, sir, up and dressed the ready and the bath not drawn." Yours truly speaking: "Never mind the bath, steward, get me a couple of fried eggs and a cup of coffee." Steward reenters with coffee and says: "You seem in a bit of a hurry this morning, sir." And I answer: "Yes, steward, I have something very important to do today. I am going to look at some frames and some deck beams."

Now, lest some of my readers should think I have spoken disparagingly of the larger steam yachts, I must correct this impression. Instead I look upon them (and they are most all gone now) as the last symbol of a seagoing people to whom romance and beauty were the principal objects of the design. They were near perfection, especially those designed by Watson, and besides having an indescribable grace, they were about the best sea boats for their size ever built. It was quite befitting that their cabins should have been carried out in the grand style for, like a statue or monument, the whole must be in keeping to acquire perfection. All I am trying to say is that I don't care about living on them any more than I would like to live in a statue.

This reminds me of an incident that Cellini, the sculptor, tells in his memoirs. It seems he had recently cast the upper part of one of his hollow bronze figures. It had been set up in the yard for finishing. One evening to better admire his handiwork Cellini was walking around it quite wrapped in admiration when, strange to say, the statue began to giggle and finally he heard soft voices. What, ho, thought he; has my statue come to life? But on closer examination it seemed one of his apprentices had decided to spend the evening there and, fearing lest the time might pass slowly, he had up with him a certain lusty wench of the neighborhood. Cellini does not tell us how they got in, but it must have been a carefully planned procedure for there was, as you can guess, scarcely room to turn around there.

This in its turn brings back to my memory a story which used to go around in my youth (for the cutter was then still in vogue). It seems there was a very small cutter somewhere on the sound, and as might be expected she was also very narrow. You would think this was a fine chance for single-handed cruising but, strange to say, the owner did not relish sailing alone so he took a certain girlfriend along with him and, as the story goes, when they went below she backed down facing aft while he followed her facing forward, for there was scarcely space to turn around in such narrow quarters. I suppose I must explain to some of my readers that this procedure was so they would be facing each other at table.

So you see there is a great difference in cabin plans and the way they are used. Yes, the cabin plan of a yacht is the most difficult part of the whole design. The reason for it is that most owners actually live on board in a very different way from the way they had planned or, perhaps I should say, dreamed. So they are very little help with the cabin plans, particularly most owners' wives. I recall one quite well. She was one of those highly refined souls whom you are continually scared of offending. She was quite troublesome when it came to arranging the cabin and chose the color scheme and upholstery herself so it would be in keeping with her personality. But the first time the yacht was in the open water the charming lady was violently seasick over the bed covering, cushions, and carpet of the after stateroom. I must admit her choice of color had given me a similar sensation.

Yes, most people cease to be normal when on a yacht under way, and the designer must always keep that fact in the back of his mind when working on the cabin plan. It may be easy to judge a person's personality or peculiarities as you see him in the office, but to hazard a guess as to how he will act at sea is quite different. You know a doctor on shore keeps a card file where he notes down certain peculiarities of his patients; he has certain symbols or letters which stand for the controlling symptoms. The letters may, for instance, be HC for hypochondriac; EX for exhibitionist, etc., for these men have to deal with the truth. It is my advice to the young yacht designer to start such a file and get well acquainted with the commonest symptoms and ailments, then study their treatment. Some of the commonest types you will run up against are gluttons, exhibitionists, imitators, and perfectionists. Perhaps you will not care for these names and can think of more appropriate ones to use. Of course, there are other types, but they never give trouble. You can call them the sensible, experienced, truthful, and well-balanced, but they are quite rare.

As for the gluttons, you must handle them most carefully. If you should suggest reducing the icebox or size of the galley, they will become quite alarmed. To see the expression on their faces you would think you had suggested leaving out the stem or the mast step or the ballast. Sometimes I say to myself, "By golly, this man's stomach is going to make the cruise single-handed; his eyes, ears, and nose and even his soul are to be left on the beach or to spend the summer in some stuffy apartment."

The exhibitionists are even more common, for we all suffer a little from that malady, but you can usually please them with paint, putty, chromium plating, and tinsel. None of them cares for boats or the sea, but only use their yachts as a moving exhibit of their wealth or their smartness. They have no interest in things like floor timbers or the lower planking, although some go in for red-stained mahogany topsides. They are tickled pink with teak rail caps, coamings, and hatchways, but the main frame of the yacht can be made of any old trash as long as it is painted or covered. Of late years these exhibitionists have gone in for mechanical gadgets, particularly below deck. Of course they get their thrill from causing astonishment, so they wire and electrify the whole cabin until it no longer resembles a yacht but looks like some boy scouts' clubroom. Perhaps they were frustrated in youth and could not play with electrical things all they wanted. Perhaps they are secretly hoping to shock someone with their electrical gadgets. However, I fear they are the ones who will be shocked when some experienced sailor tells them what he thinks of them and their electrical cabins.

The imitators are a queer lot, and you should help them if you can, for they are quite unhappy. Every time they see a Root berth, ship-to-ship telephone, or a swordfisherman's hat they must have one at once or

they are quite unhappy. When you are trying to work out a cabin plan for
them, they make up great lists of things which other people have had and
send you clippings of every advertised gadget. Yes, they must have
them all—all jammed into the cabin at once—or they will never rest
happy. The poor fellows are even worse off on deck, for if they should
see some yacht set a purple balloon jib, it may be a whole week of torture
before they can imitate it. It seems their mentality was arrested in
childhood, perhaps at the period when they were playing that game
Follow the Leader, for they are incapable of an original thought.

In racing, the imitators sometimes do quite well if they have an
Adams to follow. I have known them to come in second on several
occasions, but when they try to follow the whole class for some
psychological reason they come in quite last. Some of these imitators
who go in for cruising would undoubtedly follow *Rudder* if it steered a
good course, for it is our oldest yachting magazine. While perhaps not as
old as all of the Adams', still it has a certain veneration and should be
worth following. But it is the function of a good rudder to keep us on a
proper and sensible course. This is much more difficult today than it was
of yore, for there have sprung up innumerable uncharted shoals and
dangers to navigation. Whole reefs of laminated wood, plastics, and
wooden nutmegs. As for diesel engines, they now turn 'em out like
pancakes in some Detroit ovens. They are hot stuff all right, but I advise
the consumer to let them cool some before biting. Yes, *Rudder* should
guide us, but much will depend on the man at the helm. If he would show
us the real object of cruising, I am sure there would be less expense,
disappointment, and tragedy. If he would explain that the object of
cruising is to make a complete change of surroundings, a change for the
eyes, ears, and nose, he might make us understand why a cabin should
be very different from a city apartment—in short, explain that you
should not lug along what you are trying to leave behind. If he would
show them that there is something in life besides the stomach, organs of
reproduction, and fear, he would be doing something.

Some of our younger friends who have been reading Freud will
say, "Well, what else is there?" Now, for the want of a better word I
will call it the soul, and this will make them laugh. But the soul is
something you either have or don't have. Where it is missing, the body's
only interests are eating, drinking, and lust. Their fears are mostly the
dread of losing body comforts. When the soul is present, the person can
get along with very little indeed; he can accomplish most anything he

tries and can understand that a cabin can be built around something other than a radio, a cocktail shaker, and an icebox.

The perfectionists are quite a different lot. Sometimes I sympathize with them at first, but in the end you will find them the most troublesome of all, for nothing will quite suit them. They seem to have forgotten entirely that day off Thatcher's when the northeaster struck us butt-end foremost. It had been a warm June afternoon with a light offshore breeze, but overcast. We had passed Thatcher's and were headed between Straitsmouth and the Dry Salvages. We had expected to be anchored in Rockport, Maine, for supper, God willing, sail and power, so the owner's wife, a brave little soul but a perfectionist, was preparing a meal the boys would remember. She had planned three or four courses and had set the table and made up some salads. The yacht was a small schooner of about 50 feet on deck; she had been fitted out very carefully and I might say expensively. I remember she had a large quantity of Quimper china. Well, when the squall struck, it came with a smother of rain and shut us right in. We couldn't even see Straitsmouth, so we fetched her about and stood out to the eastward. Anybody who has sailed that coast will know why. First, we shoved all the deck clutter below—cushions, sport clothes, cocktail shaker, and all—and banged the hatch closed, for it was raining great guns. It now took on to blow in earnest, so we muzzled her jib and took in the mainsail. There was nothing to do now but run back to Gloucester, a matter of some eight miles to leeward. Well, the northeaster turned to a regular gale with plenty of cold rain. Of course, we had been too busy to put on oilskins and so were wet through to the skin. Then the owner dived below first chance he got to see how his wife was making out. The mess he saw must have been frightful. Of course, I couldn't leave the wheel to have a look at it but had to depend on later description. It seems the best part of a four-course meal was scattered over the floor, together with a lot of broken china and most of the pots, kettles, and pans off the galley, plus all the deck gear we had hove below. Well, his wife had started to clean things up but somehow slipped and fallen, cutting her knee badly on the broken glass and china. They bandaged her up but she had lost quite a little blood and, poor soul, in a moment of weakness had also lost her lunch. The owner, being a sympathetic fellow, soon followed suit. Well, all this time I was at the helm, scudding to the southwest under all the foresail could stand. The only help I had was a young man from the city, who had done most of his cruising in books. He was one of that kind who kept seeing things and would near drive you crazy. We were traveling about 8 knots and could hardly see a dozen lengths ahead in the rain. I thought by this time we should be abreast of Eastern Point, so bore in to the northwest. Now we were traveling too fast to be safe for the visibility, so I had the young man take in the foresail and start up the motor so we could feel our way in.

In the meantime, with the sea and gale on our beam, we did some great gyrating. I admit I had to hang on at the wheel, and had the young man safe in the cockpit. Down below when she took a deep roll now and then it sounded as if all "pandelorum" was let loose. We made the breakwater after a while and, when a quarter of a mile to weather of Dog Bar, came to anchor. Now this is none too sheltered a place, but I was too cold, wet, and tired to go on any farther. I intended to dive below, have a drink, and then get out the second anchor, for it was now screeching a full gale. Well, I went below and could hardly believe my eyes. Everything movable lay in a heap on the cabin sole—food, books, broken china, and all. Under all this ran a red liquid—seemed enough blood for a slaughtered ox. It was real blood (some of it) with tomato soup, catsup, and seasickness.

The yacht had one of those improved stoves that don't give off any heat. It was cold enough on deck—wet through to the skin, God knows—but down here it seemed worse. My friend of the books had stripped off and turned in. The owner and his wife were in the forward stateroom in bed. It was the only thing you could do to get warm. After my drink I was real hungry, for it was long past suppertime. I found a can of sardines and some bread that wasn't too red. Now I once had a pretty tough stomach, but that cabin was too much for me. I just took the can opener and went down in the forepeak. If you have been real hungry and cold you can imagine those sardines tasted like ambrosia, and they sure did, but I had a shivering fit and could hardly eat them. After I let the second anchor go, I stripped off, rubbed down, took another drink, and turned in. Nothing could have stopped me; if she had gone ashore, I would have stayed right in the bunk. If some of you have been really cold, you can understand me. It was a long time before I could go to sleep for shivering. As I lay there, I thought to myself, "Here's a cabin cost about four thousand dollars and hardly a foot of it fit to live in." Yes, when you really need a cabin or shelter, you need it bad. Give me a simple one with coal-burning stove every time.

Some of my readers will say, "Oh, yes, poor seamanship," or perhaps, "It's a foul bird that litters its nest." But I don't know—those squalls without warning strike once or twice a year. If one strikes you on a rocky lee shore, you'll do about as we did. The point is, a cabin should be designed for emergencies and be as foolproof as possible, entirely free of anything that can get loose or under foot in a knockdown.

Speaking of cabins reminds me of a night I spent once in Buzzards Bay. In my younger days I liked to deliver some of the new small sailboats built by the Herreshoff Manufacturing Company at Bristol. This time it was one of their 14^1/$_2$-footers. It was when they first came out. Well, they are chunky little vessels and rather good sailers, but we had a calm for about forty-eight hours (it was in the dog days of August). The first night we put in behind the breakwater at Sakonnet, but every room in the inn there was taken, so I slept on some life preservers spread out on her grating. This was all right, but on toward morning I thought it would be quite as comfortable under way. No one was up in the inn, so I put to sea without any breakfast. Well, it turned out one of those grayish-brown days with a glassy sea and now and then a light shower. I had an oar out most of the time but didn't round the spindle on the Old Cock till somewhere around noontime. It was so calm you could hear the factory whistles at New Bedford. I don't care much about rowing a boat with one hand and steering with the other, but it was one of those cases where you had to make up your mind to like it, so I rowed all afternoon, in fact until dark; then, feeling rather weak (no breakfast, dinner, or supper), I determined to have a rest, so came to anchor in the shallow water off West Island not far from the middle of Buzzards Bay. No sooner had I snugged down for the night than it started to thunder and lighten. It was one of those all-night thunderstorms we have in the summer without much wind but now and then a heavy shower. Well, if you spend the night alone in an open boat in a thunderstorm, it will do a couple of things to you—it will bring you closer to God than going to church forty Sundays. Yes, and it will make you talk reason about cabin plans. If you have really needed a cabin once, you will know what it is all about. A tight deck, a dry place for some food, a berth, and a lamp to read by are the main things; sometimes the very small cabin or cuddy is the nicest.

I suppose now, man and boy, I have slept a thousand nights on yachts. These yachts and boats may number a hundred; they range from steam yachts and the large racing sailers down to open boats—some of them were the finest yachts ever built. I had an opportunity in my youth to listen to the conversation of a father [Nathanael] who had designed over two thousand yachts. I have watched or inspected the construction of literally hundreds that were all different, and studied their cabin layouts. Twenty years ago I used to think I knew something about cabin plans but now, with fifty years' experience with them, I feel differently. But a cabin can usually be simplified; if it can, my advice to you is—do it!

Sometimes when quite young I used to start on a trip with very little. The principal reason was that I usually left the boat or yacht with its new owner and came home overland by horse and wagon, trolley car, or steam train. My father, who had had exhaustive experience in cruising (for he started at it about 1858), never showed disapproval of this Spartan simplicity, but I can remember several times as I was about to start off he came down to the wharf and said, "Now, Francis, don't forget to take along some drinking water." I suppose there had been some time in his past when he had even forgotten this necessity in his hurry to get sailing.

One time about 1904, I remember we had just come to anchor in the New Harbor at Block Island. We were on my father's steam yacht *Roamer*. I was in the pilot house with my father and said, "Oh, look at the beautiful little yacht over there." "Yes," said my father (and he was a man of few words), "that should be Captain Arthur Clark on the *Minerva*. If you will bring the dinghy to the starboard gangway without bumping her, I will let you row me over to call." Now the *Minerva* was the prettiest thing I had ever seen, and when I say "pretty" I mean it; and I still think so. Many yachts are handsome, graceful, or beautiful, but when it comes to pretty—well, a flower, a young girl, and sometimes a tern are pretty. But the *Minerva* was not only pretty, she had crossed the Atlantic on her own bottom and cleaned up the 40-foot class in 1889. You can imagine I pulled smartly on the oars, expecting to get a glimpse of her cabin. After the formalities were over (and these two full-bearded men well in their 60s could leave many things unsaid, for they understood each other), we went below. Well, if the *Minerva* was pretty on deck, below she was decidedly plain—only a little paint work, the rest as I remember it being mostly scrubbed elm, that wood which turns whiter with scrubbing.

The best way I can describe her now is to say she looked well-worn—she had undoubtedly had more than a thousand scrubbings. I am now going to try and tell you some scraps of the conversation between these two men, for it might help you in designing a cabin, but first I should tell you something about who they were.

Captain Arthur Hamilton Clark had written "The Clipper Ship

Era'' and ''The History of Yachting,'' the best books on these subjects ever written. He had sailed out to China at the age of 17. He soon rose in rank and at 22 had a master's certificate and a ship of his own. He later commanded several ships in the China trade, including some of the first steamers to undertake this long voyage. Captain Clark had retired from the sea when about 35 and had since represented various marine insurance companies and been a commissioner representing America in the Alabama claims. In his residence in various parts of the world he had collected perhaps one of the best privately owned collections of pictures of shipping and craft, and at the time of which we speak was Lloyd's agent for the port and district of New York and one of the greatest authorities on maritime matters in the United States. He had crossed the Atlantic twice on yachts, and to my way of thinking was a handsome man.

As for my father, maybe I can best describe him for the present purpose by saying he had perhaps designed more cabin plans than any man who had ever lived, but he was a man of very few words.

I have said *Minerva*'s cabin was plain; it consisted of two berths, two transom seats with cushions, a table, and some books, well secured. No doubt forward she had a galley and forecastle, probably two or more hands. There was absolutely nothing could have gotten loose in a knockdown. As we sat down my father said, ''You look mighty comfortable here.'' Now Captain Clark understood what he meant, but in case you don't, I'll translate it. He meant, ''I don't see a lot of damn foolishness in this cabin that will be more trouble than it is worth.'' Captain Clark said, ''Yes, I am having about the best time of my life. I love the *Minerva*, and I've got some books with me.'' I think you can translate this last; but if you can't, you will *never* understand cabins.

The Ideal
Blue-Water Boat

by Tom Colvin

DECEMBER, 1969

Tom Colvin's first design was an 18-foot gaff-rigged sloop, drawn in 1936; since then, he's designed at least a hundred more. At one time he was senior designer at Newport News Shipyard. Here, he makes the case for an engineless 42-foot junk-rigged schooner with Spartan accommodations.

My ideal blue-water cruising sailboat was to be above all comfortable, seaworthy, seakindly, fast, and easily handled—requirements based on a series of intended voyages which included non-stop passages, the shortest some 600 miles, the longest, 3,500 miles. She was also to be suitable for day sailing, weekend sailing, and general cruising in my home waters, Chesapeake Bay.

What sort of vessel meets all these requirements?

In my case, a lug-rigged steel schooner, 42 feet on deck and 33 on the waterline, with 11-foot-4½ beam and 3-foot-10 draft. Her displacement is 18,000 pounds, of which 7,500 is ballast, and her sail area is 854 square feet on the wind and 1,203 square feet off the wind. Each of these factors is important, so let's investigate them all.

First, I am not speaking of a vessel on which my family of five would live with any permanence. I consider a 30- to 36-foot waterline length the smallest on which five could cruise with any comfort, and only when all five belong to the same family. But if the habits of the owner tend toward simplicity, as mine do, it is possible to have a fine, light-displacement blue-water cruiser on that waterline at a rather modest cost. My experience with light and ultra-light displacement has been quite favorable, so I had little hesitation in returning to the type for my new boat. Light displacement permits one to have a much larger vessel for a given displacement, resulting in longer waterline, more boat speed, and more linear room on the interior. Surprisingly, for a given displacement the internal cube varies very little; a short, fat, deep boat has about the same cubic as that of a long, lean, shoal vessel, but is not nearly as comfortable or as fast. My *Gazelle* is long, lean, and light.

An engine does, in spite of what many think, influence the design of the hull, the concept of the rig, and one's general approach to cruising. One advantage of *not* having an engine aboard is never having to think about it. Careful planning can eliminate most of the noise and smell of an engine, but omitting it entirely reduced the cost of maintenance and eventual replacement, not to mention the initial cost of the engine and installation. Propeller and aperture drag—which slows up the vessel more than one may realize—is also quite important. With no propeller dragging, any boat sails faster. During my thirty-eight years of sailing, I have owned but one vessel with an auxiliary. It was used about one-half of one percent of the time—a dubious convenience for the expense involved. Most important, once an auxiliary is installed, even the best of sailors will subconsciously depend on it in an emergency and use it when sail and good, alert seamanship should suffice. Most of the accidents I have seen involving stranding or loss of vessel have been caused by failure of the engine to start or to accomplish what good seamanship would have dictated be done under sail alone. Moreover, I maintain that there are few, if any, ports in the world that cannot be entered under sail, using only patience, wind, sea, and tide.

By not having an engine on *Gazelle*, we have a wonderful cargo hold. By not having a cockpit, it is even larger. Stores can be placed in readily accessible compartments and bins instead of below the cabin sole. Access to the hold is from both cabins, so it also makes an excellent hanging locker for shore-going clothes; there are four hanging lockers elsewhere on this vessel.

My wife is neither physically strong nor large enough to do a man's work, and I do not expect her to—she just says I do. Taking care of the children (ages 12, 8, and 6), preparing meals, plus doing her trick at the wheel are more than her share of the voyage. So for all practical purposes, the vessel must be a single-hander. And personally, I would not own a vessel I couldn't sail alone with ease.

There are few vessels that can match a schooner for efficiency, and the rig is so easily handled that one can tend lots of sail with a very small crew—namely me. Topsails and a powerful fisherman or main topmast staysail can be set for fine reaching performance, and multiple masts allow more combinations of heavy-weather sail distribution with less effort, a definite plus in ocean cruising. Another plus is *Gazelle*'s Chinese lug rig, which I've found not only efficient and easy to handle but surprisingly inexpensive in initial cost and maintenance.

For a light-displacement vessel, our *Gazelle* is not at all stingy with sail, and she does well on all points of sailing in all weather up to Force 8. Her narrow beam necessitates reefing for comfort by the time Force 5 is reached, but that's easily done because numerous combinations are available since the lugsail's battens are lowered one by one. Because of its extreme flatness and control of all the battens from deck, the lug rig is good both on and off the wind. If we also assume that, for ocean cruising, the closest anyone would choose to sail would be five points or more to the wind, why stress the ability to point higher at the sacrifice of efficiency, ease of handling, and efficiency on other points of sailing?

The question of lee shores immediately arises. I have been "caught" on lee shores many times, both by error and by intent. To work off one requires the ability to carry sail—lots of it—plus a vessel that sails well and won't sag off in tacking. Even so, under some conditions a vessel the size of *Gazelle* may not be able to weather the lee shore; anchoring or running her ashore may be the only solutions.

With regard to anchoring, modern anchor designs make it possible to use lighter anchor weights, but in practice the necessity of more chain and greater scope to insure sufficient holding power add up to about the same total weight as the old-fashioned yachtsman or kedge anchor, which *Gazelle* carries, stowed on her foredeck. The advantage of the older anchors is that while they may be more difficult to stow and to handle, it is possible to anchor in three times the depth of water, opening many anchorages too cramped for use with lightweight anchors. And, if stowed on the foredeck, it is possible to get a second anchor down in very tight anchorages. Provisions can be made to prevent jibsheets from fouling deck-stowed anchors under way.

Similarly, the advantages of *Gazelle*'s shoal draft easily outweigh its drawbacks of reduced stability and less-than-breathtaking windward performance. The thousands of interesting places in the world with less than one fathom of water easily justify shoal draft.

All blue-water sailing vessels are, in effect, cargo carriers. In order to be self-sustaining, the vessel must carry, in addition to her crew and normal cruising gear, much larger quantities of food, water, linen, clothing, books, charts, spare parts, and various other supplies. I usually figure eight pounds per day per person to be ample for cruising. This allows each person five pounds of water (maximum) and three pounds of food and consumable personal items per day.

As far as navigational equipment is concerned, I concede that many modern instruments are good and even convenient. I do doubt their long-term reliability. For shoal water, I use a sounding pole. For deeper water, a sounding lead, armed if necessary. I also prefer a taffrail log, as it can be streamed only when desired, then oiled and stowed in its box, where it should have almost unlimited life. Though I do carry a radio direction finder, I still use the old time-sight method most of the time.

I believe that it is a mistake to design a hull around an interior, but at the same time, I recognize that the necessities of rudimentary comfort must be taken into account. The idea of a double bunk is appealing, but I like to have an additional sea berth for heavy weather—one that is snug and can be slept in without undue tossing about.

We will use both coal and Primus kerosene stoves in the galley. My wife likes a double sink in the galley and a basin in the head. Speaking of heads, our two are the self-contained, hand-operated chemical type (glorified cedar buckets), which comply with present regulations. As a result, there are no through-hull fittings below the waterline and only three above it—two sink outlets and a bilge pump discharge. Happily, my family does not need or desire an icebox or refrigerator, luxury gear which would only complicate an otherwise simple and convenient layout. For those who desire one, there is an excellent kerosene-operated refrigerator on the market which, with slight modification, can be made serviceable for a sailing vessel.

We also have no electricity—the RDF and binnacle light are battery-powered, and our lights are candle lamps or kerosene lamps which have been faithful cruising companions for many years. Because of my belief in adequate ventilation, there are twenty-two opening portholes in *Gazelle*, one skylight, and three hatches, two of which are companionways.

For ease of maintenance and reliability, we used painted heavy-wall aluminum pipe for spars and bowsprit. We also use galvanized-iron standing rigging for long-term reliability (no stress corrosion), greased or oiled three or four times a year. We use deadeyes and lanyards which do not freeze or corrode. All running rigging is dacron.

The hull of *Gazelle*, constructed of 10-gauge Cor-ten steel for strength and light weight, had been sandblasted and metalized with molten aluminum prior to painting. Access around the cabin trunk on deck is excellent because there is only one fitting, a pad eye, on the side decks. Cleats and belaying pins are either mounted on the rail aft, on the raised deck at the break, or on the side of the cabin trunk. With the possibility of grounding in mind, I find it convenient to have a hand-operated capstan on the foredeck, better than a windlass because it can lead fair through 360 degrees. *Gazelle*'s two homemade halyard winches are very simply constructed and permit both main and foresail to be reefed without uncoiling and recoiling the halyards. The winch axles are made from Volkswagen wheel spindles, encased in permanently grease-packed watertight housings, bolted to the forward and aft ends of the cabin trunk.

What about results of this dream design? The rig has proven to be beyond my greatest expectations. She balances on all points of sailing, requires no one at the wheel under most conditions, and needs only minor attention when running off in heavy weather. The schooner is at a disadvantage dead before the wind, for unless she is wing-and-wing, the mainsail blankets the foresail so the hull is really being driven by the mainsail alone. In light weather this is of little consequence, but in stronger airs it can lead to a heavy helm. With lug rigs the main blankets the foresail even more than on a conventional schooner, so while it is possible to use preventers to go wing-and-wing up to Force 4 or 5, we increase our speed so much by sailing off a couple of points that it more than justifies not running dead before the wind. On all other points of sailing, regardless of weather conditions, *Gazelle* is self-steering or can be made to self-steer. She carries about two spokes of lee helm in light weather, neutral helm at about Force 3 or 4, and two spokes of weather helm in Force 5 and 6 winds.

As to hull form, there is little to be desired. She is extremely easily driven and very fast. Under foresail and jib, close-reaching, she's done 8 knots for several hours at a time. From calm to Force 4 winds, we sailed 48 nautical miles at 3.5 knots in absolute comfort. Reaching, under ideal conditions with Force 5 winds, we averaged 8.9 knots between buoys of 2.5 miles, though she was becoming heavy at the helm, and we even surfed her once, but we can't know her exact speed. Throughout a variety of conditions, I can predict consistent 125-mile days with *Gazelle*.

As to stability, *Gazelle* likes 10 to 15 degrees of heel. She hardens up at 18 to 20 degrees, and it would take more wind than we have had to bury her rail. She's proven she can be driven hard to windward when others were using power for the same job—in spite of her shoal draft, she has more than enough lateral plane.

Gazelle was built in a year of my spare time; however, materials had been collected for almost three years before, and a number of items incorporated in her are from other vessels I have owned.

The cost of materials can be broken down as follows: steel, $2,000; spar material, $500; interior joiner woods, linoleum, etc., $800; stoves, sinks, toilets, interior lamps, mattresses, and cushions, $1,000; four water tanks and piping, running lights, rigging, steering gear, compass, and ventilators, $1,500; sand-blasting, metalizing, and interior and exterior painting, $1,500; portlights, screens, and hatches, $500; dinghy and davits, $650. Between 3,000 and 4,000 man-hours of labor were involved in construction and outfitting. The sails are of 10-ounce Vivatex and cost less than $100 for material, including the dacron thread, plus $50 for bolt ropes and grommets and 100 hours of my time to loft and sew them. With labor at $5 to $6 an hour, it was possible to build my ideal blue-water sailboat, equip and ready her for sea, for under $30,000.

Fast, cheap, and fully found, that's my *Gazelle*. There are no frills, a few conveniences, and a few of my own weaknesses indulged. By "modern" standards, the sailors we meet must think we're still sailing in the Middle Ages. But we're able to sail immediately and at any time from here to the other side of almost any ocean quickly and comfortably. To me, that's what a blue-water boat is all about.

Three Designers: I.
Olin Stephens 2nd

by Stafford Huntington

SEPTEMBER, 1934

By the end of the third race of the 1974 America's Cup contest, it had become clear that the Australian's "unbeatable" challenger, Southern Cross, *was no match for* Courageous. *The American boat pointed higher and simply walked away. After the Australian boat had dragged across the line more than five minutes behind* Courageous, *a crew member on the losing boat stood up, raised his hands, and shrugged as if to say, "There's no way to beat that boat."*

There were several victors that day, none more venerable than Courageous' *designer, Olin Stephens 2nd. After the finish he wore the same toothy grin, the same kind of studious spectacles that were his trademark more than 40 years ago. This portrait shows that even in*

1934, at 26, Stephens had established himself as one of the country's master designers.

To few men in any profession is vouchsafed the experience of swarming up the shrouds to the masthead of success in less time than was required to obtain the necessary technical background for the climb. Still more of a rarity is the feat of remaining aloft after such a rapid rise, despite the obvious perils of the position. To do so requires unusual ability, a modicum of luck, a great deal of courage, and, perhaps, a touch of genius.

Olin J. Stephens 2nd, an outstanding naval architect at the age of 26 with a lustrous record of achievement in all phases of the business, is an illustration of the point.

An innate love of boats developed by a boyhood spent afloat in racing and cruising craft led to a course in naval architecture at Massachusetts Institute of Technology. A fortuitous dinner date with Drake H. Sparkman, who had faith in the youth's possibilities and was willing to gamble, provided the necessary break. Courage to tackle the design of yachts in the toughest of racing classes, backed by a genuine gift for laying down the lines for fast boats, took care of the rest.

His slips have been negligible; his successes above the average. Forty boats of all types for a wide variety of purposes have sprung to life from his drawing board and carried his name wherever men go down to the sea for sport or pleasure. He has designed everything from sailing dinghies to ocean-going cruising vessels, from rowboats to fancy, luxurious power craft. The day does not appear far distant when he will be called in to create a defender, or maybe a challenger, for the America's Cup, the dream of every naval architect.

After his studies at M.I.T., Stephens, then a none-too-robust lad peering at the world through spectacles under a shock of curly, light hair and speaking in a quiet, low-toned voice that revealed his shyness and modesty, went into the office of Henry J. Gielow, Inc., as a draftsman. Poor health necessitated the abandonment of this orthodox start toward a career.

In the summer of 1928, a year after Drake Sparkman had gone into the yacht brokerage business on his own, Olin and his father had dinner with the broker at the Larchmont Yacht Club. During the meal Olin told of his ambition to become a yacht designer. Sparkman had known Olin as a youngster who cruised on the little sloop *Scrapper* and the able if somewhat ponderous ketch *Sou'wester*. He was familiar with his racing at the stick of *Alicia*, the family's Sound schooner, and *Natka*, one of the better 6-meter sloops.

Sparkman played a hunch. He felt that the boy had that intangible something that makes the difference between mediocrity and flaming success. He suggested an informal partnership for a year, and terms were agreed upon.

That winter, Arthur P. Hatch of Stamford, Connecticut, was persuaded to entrust Stephens, then utterly unknown in the field, with the design of a small auxiliary sloop. The result was *Kalmia*, which went into the 1929 Gibson Island race and won in her class. When *Kalmia* was taking form, the Junior Yacht Racing Association of Long Island Sound conceived the idea of sponsoring a one-design knockabout of modern type that would provide fast, comfortable, and safe racing for youngsters. Stephens went to work, and what he turned out is as sweet and easily-handled a small racing boat as any boy or girl could desire.

By that time—the spring of 1929—Sparkman was convinced that he had not erred in his judgment of the studious, diffident lad he had picked up off the beach instead of shipping a more seasoned, better-known hand. So the partnership was made permanent, but the formalities of organizing the firm of Sparkman & Stephens, Inc., had to wait until Olin reached his twenty-first birthday that autumn.

During the winter of 1929-30, Stephens designed the fine little cruising cutters *Cynara* and *Salabar*; the jib-headed, 30-rater sloop *Alsumar* for Dave Henen Morris, Jr., and the now famous yawl *Dorade* for himself.

Dorade and Stephens are synonymous in the world of yachting. The feats of this amazing yacht are high spots in ocean-racing history. *Dorade* has repeatedly shown herself not only to be a fast offshore boat but an exceptionally able one. In the Bermuda race of 1930, Olin and his brother, Roderick, Jr., got *Dorade* to the "Onion Patch" so fast that she took second prize in class B. In 1931 she walloped a distinguished fleet of ocean racers in the long haul from Newport, Rhode Island, to Plymouth, England, and topped this brilliant performance by winning the Fastnet race.

She went to Bermuda again in 1932 and won in her class. A year later she made a notable cruise to Norway and paused on her way home long enough to carry the Stars and Stripes to victory again in her second thrash through the stormy Fastnet race. Olin's brother, Roderick, who was in charge of *Dorade* that season, was awarded the Blue Water Medal for his superior seamanship.

Last year, just about the nadir in yachting activity due to the prevailing business conditions, saw Stephens turn his hand to creating the modern power cruiser *El Nido* for Everett Dickinson of Essex, Connecticut, and step into the motor-sailer field with the 65-footer *Tamerlane* for George B. Knowles of New Bedford. *Tamerlane* is a refutation of the oft-heard assertion that motor-sailers are nothing but clumsy buckets under sail. *Tamerlane* has repeatedly proved that she can step along under her tall ketch rig and carry it to windward far better than one would expect of a yacht of this type.

With business better and yachtsmen loosening up their purse strings, the 1933-34 season was another of persistent activity for the junior member of the firm of Sparkman & Stephens. He turned out an 11-foot sailing dinghy which the Larchmont Yacht Club adopted as a means of teaching the rising generation how to sail, a 65-foot motor-sailer for Clarence Postley, two 30-foot Duxbury Yacht Club one-design auxiliaries, the auxiliary ketch *Roon III*, the auxiliary cutter *Aweigh*, the auxiliary yawl *Blue Heron*, and the 70-foot auxiliary cruising yawl *Alsumar* for Dave Henen Morris, Jr.

He also worked up the designs for *Stormy Weather*, a slightly larger and improved *Dorade*-type yawl, for Philip Le Boutillier, and the cruising sloop *Edlu* in which Rudolph J. Schaefer, rear-commodore of Larchmont, won the Bermuda race.

This summer, besides watching the tuning up of his latest creations, he has served in the afterguard of the America's Cup candidate *Weetamoe* and applied himself to learning things about class J cutters that will be invaluable one of these days.

He can design a boat and he can sail one, this amazing young man who at 26 can look back on achievements worthy of a naval architect of twice his age and five times his experience.

Three Designers: II.
John Hanna

John G. Hanna designed tough, roomy, double-ended ketch-rigged boats to carry their owners long distances, often around the world. Tahiti ketches alone—built from Hanna's design for the double-ended 30-footer—have made at least half a dozen circumnavigations.

Hanna drew his boats in Dunedin, Florida, where he could watch the growth of watery traffic year-round. He didn't like all that he saw, and in 1929, began contributing his philosophy to Rudder *in a regular column called "The Watch Below."*

Not since Thomas Fleming Day's fulminations had the magazine printed such irascible, often funny, copy. These excerpts are taken from Hanna's columns from 1931 to 1941.

The most interesting thing to me in the last issue was the symposium of opinions on the best rig for offshore cruising. And what struck me forcibly was not the differences in minor particulars, but the almost unanimous agreement of all these authorities on the broad fundamentals. With scarcely an exception, all of these experienced men agree that the ketch is the most desirable rig for the smaller craft and the schooner for larger sizes. Also, while the Marconi sail gets some good words for the smaller ketches and for the main of small schooners, the gaff rig has the solid backing of three out of four men cruising, not racing. This entitles me to a smile or two, I hope, seeing it was only a few years ago that the boys were writing indignant letters to the editor because JGH refused to concede that the gaff was not utterly obsolete for everything but lumber schooners. Another point I note with pleasure is that most of these designers have the same profound contempt for the yawl I had held all my life. (Note to editor: prepare for broadside of abuse from all owners of yawls.) The undeniable historical fact is that the yawl is simply an outgrowth of the sloop, and was invented in the days of excessively long sloop booms. Old-timers can remember when no sloop was considered fashionable enough to belong to a yacht club if its boom did not extend 10 to 30 feet aft of the transom. It was simply taking the slightly lesser of two evils to cut off this excess and put on a jigger. Nowadays, when higher sails with shorter booms are universally recognized as more efficient, there seems no excuse for designing yawls.

But I am afraid that, since thinking is an unknown art to most yachtsmen, the real meat of these articles, buried in a few unobtrusive sentences here and there, will be entirely overlooked. For instance, [Ralph] Winslow says, "By cruiser I do *not* mean a racer." And the bitter truth is, four out of every five yachtsmen who ask an architect to design a cruiser, *do* want a racer, and heaven pity the poor architect if he does not deliver just that. He is in for a lot of dirty sneers if he doesn't. And [Winthrop] Warner says, "I believe that fully 75 percent of the people who inquire regarding the merits of various rigs for offshore cruising do not really mean it in the true sense of the word. The majority of them are talking about a safe rig for coastal cruising which, after all, is an entirely different proposition." Yea, verily! And [J. Murray] Watts says, "In real heavy wind and sea a yacht cannot make much progress close-hauled to windward and most of the actual cruising is done with the wind free." Now isn't it about time to admit that? Every cruising yacht built nowadays, whatever the rig, has an engine. And you know and I know and everybody knows that they practically always step on the starter for windward work, excepting only in races in which engines are barred. Isn't it about time cruisers quit sacrificing everything to the racer's prime essential, good windward performance, and began designing expressly for good performance in sailing free, the only kind of sailing they ever do? For it is a well-known fact that a crack windward racer is the most dangerous thing that can be designed for running before heavy seas. Few ever dare this most exhilarating point of sailing. Heaving-to is their only safety then.

* * *

In proof of my assertion that thinking is an unknown process to most yachtsmen. I can give you a thousand facts, but will present only one instance, right hot off the griddle. *Scimitar III* [a Hanna design entered in the 1931 St. Petersburg-to-Cuba race] reached Havana thirty-two hours after the crack racer *Haligonian*. To date some twenty yachtsmen have given me their opinions on this matter, and each and every one is fully satisfied this is simply because *Scimitar* has a very hard-driving hull, simply because she has not a long, sharp nose. How many of these wisenheimers bothered to study the underwater lines of the hull and discover that whatever added resistance there might be forward was offset by the cleanest run aft of any vessel in the fleet, a run as clean as a Gar Wood or Chris-Craft speedboat, reducing the drag (the greatest resistance on most hulls) to the irreducible minimum? NONE. And how many experts bothered to ask what was her actual sail area, and whether slowness was the result of over-resistance or under-powering? NONE. And how many deep thinkers were aware that the boat entered this race with as foul a bottom as bottoms ever get? [*Scimitar* crew member] Blackford, who examined it after the race, tells me it was the most astounding collection of vegetable and animal life he has ever seen—and he has seen them in Rangoon, Hong Kong, Legaspi, and all points east and west. A foul bottom is known to cut the speed of even a full-powered steamship as much as 25 percent, but NONE of the deep thinkers took this into consideration. How many of them took the trouble to compare day's runs and learn that the leaders piled up most of their lead on the second day, of very light winds, when they ghosted along under their light racing kites, whereas *Scimitar* had not even a rag of spinnaker to set and made only 47 miles? NONE. And how many of the smart boys waited to hear Houston Wall [owner of *Haligonian*] say, as he said to me, that he was lucky to get in before the gale broke, and if he had had to fight it across the Stream, as *Scimitar* did, he would still have beaten her, *if* he had been able to keep his spars, but not by anywhere near such a big margin as thirty-two hours? NONE. In short, all these twenty expert yachtsmen took one look at a hull, made an instantaneous short circuit from eye to mouth and shot off a big noise, leaving their brains entirely unused. That, I suppose, is why yachting is such a popular sport. It doesn't take any brains to enjoy it.

* * *

I looked over [William Robinson's globe-circling] *Svaap* at the show with keen interest. Sorry I couldn't see the inside, as it was locked up. Not that I blame Robinson for this. If he had left it open to the crowds, souvenir hunters would not have left so much as one cockroach in it. I hunted for him for days but couldn't find him. For myself, I wouldn't pick that boat for a trip around Long Island, much less the world. It must be a very wearing strain to sit on the roof at the wheel with the tiller ropes constantly sawing at one's anatomy. Possibly bearable in the warm tropics, but mighty little shelter against cold, driving spray farther north. The deeper the water I sail on, the deeper I want my cockpit. I think too that one foot less draft would have meant far greater safety in seas full of uncharted reefs, and no detriment to sailing ability, judging by the records of several other small circumnavigating boats. But at least *Svaap* is not one-half of one percent as bad as her name—but keep your shirt on, Robinson. This is a free country, and I am only expressing one man's humble, unimportant, individual opinion. If you like it, there's no law agin it. You could even call her *Bounding Banana* if you wanted to.

* * *

Probably I am expected to state here my opinions of the America's Cup races. At least, everyone else who owns or can borrow, rent, or steal a typewriter has stated his. It is just too bad, but I will have to disappoint the cash customers. I am so completely fed up with hearing and reading entirely too many million words about this very trivial subject for the last six months that nothing could induce me to add more to the total. I prefer to look forward—a long way forward, let us hope—and offer a suggestion that may revive interest in a moribund subject. Plainly, big-sloop racing has been carried to its final limit. There never was any good reason for putting a single-stick rig on hulls 125 feet long. Everyone knows that a hull of that size rates two masts. A 125-foot sloop is merely a challenge to human ingenuity. The challenge has been fully met. The engineers have proved that they can build such things and make the junk hold together, at least in a moderate breeze.

Other boys have proved that they could sail them. Still other lads have proved that they are clever enough to get money enough to pay for them. So all hands should be satisfied, what? The trouble with all tricks is that after you have seen them a dozen times, they get to be a frightful bore. If the rule-makers consider that their dignity will not permit racing with anything smaller than 125-foot hulls, I tell them here and now that the only possible way to keep up any interest in the business is to go back to schooner rigs. And why not? A 125-foot schooner is an exceedingly practical, safe, and useful craft. Every seaman knows it takes a far higher grade of seamanship to get the best out of a two-master than a sloop. Sloops are simple enough for our youngest children to use for their first lessons. It would be better to go back to schooner racing and a man's game. The claim that the sloop is the fastest rig is simply a lot of kelp. It may be so in drifting matches, but in real sailing weather the schooner's speed inferiority, if any, is so slight that it is ridiculous to quibble and niggle about it. Enough of the toy boats. Let's have some schooner racing.

*   *   *

It is undoubtedly true that Joshua Slocum was an amazing man, and his story of his cruise around the world [from 1895-98] aboard the 37-foot *Spray* has had a great influence on landsmen ever since. Peter Culler is not the only 16-year-old boy, by hundreds, who, completely without the slightest trace of the technical education necessary to enable one to foresee the action of floating bodies of various forms, let his hero-worship and his wishful thinking delude him into believing that he "recognized Slocum's wisdom in choosing a model of a boat which would be seaworthy, comfortable, and workable for extended cruising anywhere." There is no excuse for any such conclusion, since the honest captain's book makes it perfectly clear that his choice was dictated solely by his financial limitations, and that the credit for his successful circumnavigation belongs in part to his immense resourcefulness, based on a lifetime of experience sailing everything, including square-riggers, and in part to extreme good luck in the pinches (he ascribes it to his own belief in a "guardian spirit," but whether you call it that or "good luck" is immaterial), and in no part at all to the form of his vessel. Just as in the case of that other daring, resourceful and lucky man, Thomas Fleming Day, who crossed the ocean in the little yawl *Sea*

Bird, and honestly stated in his writings a plain truth which willful self-deluders have ignored—namely, that he did not choose the ideal boat for such a trip, but simply the only boat his financial limitations would permit. Mr. Culler has selected a very good houseboat for living on the year around, and he shows most admirable judgment in "sailing" it up and down the intracoastal canal as much as possible rather than venturing outside, particularly in view of his folly in putting 6 x 8 frames in such a little hull. He, of course, does not remotely dream of what effect such disproportionate construction will have on the metacentric height of his floating log cabin, nor what that metacentric height will mean in a really nasty Gulf Stream crossing. But should he ever attempt an ocean voyage in this craft, his friends may as well kiss him good-bye.

* * *

Since the Suicide Squad has been for many years building exact copies of *Spray*, and will continue doing so for many years more unless restrained, perhaps I can save a life or two by explaining, as simply as possible, the basic reason (skipping many other good reasons) why *Spray* is the worst possible boat for anyone, and especially anyone lacking the experience and resourcefulness of Slocum, to take off soundings. It is for the same reason that the Cape Cod cat and the inland lake racing scow are not suitable for ocean going. Everyone who has handled these types knows that, though they are extremely stiff initially, if they are ever heeled beyond a critical point, they flop right over as inevitably as a soup plate, which they resemble. What a boat does in a coastal chop has no bearing on what it will do in the great waves of the deep sea. A big lurching cross sea, that would scarcely disturb a properly designed hull, can—especially if it coincides, as if often does, with an extra-savage puff of a squall—flip over a *Spray* hull just as you would a poker chip. The capsizing of one *Spray* duplicate, just off the coast of South America, was recorded in *Rudder* many years ago. Many duplicates trying to duplicate the circumnavigation have disappeared without a trace, just as the original *Spray* and Slocum did. Others have been wrecked with part or all of their crew saved in various ways. Of the great fleet that has tried in all these years, but one *Spray* duplicate ever completed the circuit—Roger Strout's *Igdrasil*. And his published accounts of his voyage indicate that throughout the greater part of it he met generally favorable weather; also that he carried an immense fuel supply (in relation to the size of his engine) and ran every possible mile under power. Moreover, in letters to this writer, he has stated that on at least two occasions his vessel was flipped up to the very point of the last roll-over, and for a second or two it seemed she would never come back on her bottom. After such experience, it is understandable that he says, if building again for such a trip, he would willingly sacrifice the much-loved comfort of broad decks and great initial stability for more of that *final* stability which infallibly rights a well-designed yacht even if knocked down with her masts in the water. I trust a little sober reflection on these facts will cause a ray of light to dawn in the minds of another generation of would-be *Spray* duplicators. The famous old ship had her good points—and no one admires them more than I—but not enough to overcome some almost certainly fatal faults.

* * *

As is well know, I am a very patient man, but I can be pushed only so far, and I have been sitting on a certain safety valve as long as I can and am ready to blow up. I don't care if you call me just an old clam-digger, or what. I admit old age is stealing up on me and I am no longer the powerful brute I once was. Nevertheless, I want to tell all you Little Lord Fauntleroys right now that I am still perfectly and entirely able to haul, with my own unaided hands, each and every rope on any little racing skimabout or tabloid cruiser, without a bit of help from a mess of organ grinders' winches, sticking up like warts all over the craft.

Three Designers: III. Uffa Fox

by Martin Luray

NOVEMBER, 1972

Luray's portrait of Britain's Grand Old Man of boating appeared the month Uffa Fox died, still searching for the perfect hull shape.

". . . But you must at all times remember that the power of the sea is greater than anything else on earth; and that although many fleets have sailed over it, not one has conquered or harnessed it, and no one ever will. Remember, too, that like fire, the sea is a good friend but a bad master; so you must never, never allow yourself to get into the position where the sea takes control."

Uffa Fox

It's possible that there are sailors in this world who have never heard of Uffa Fox. But if this is true they are not Englishmen, for this seagoing renaissance man has reigned as guru and resident genius of British small-boat sailors and powerboat designers for more years than one might think likely. For better than sixty years now, Uffa Fox has had the love-hate relationship with the sea expressed in the quote above, which comes out of one of a dozen books he has written about the practicalities of sailing, cruising, power, and sail design—and of life and living it in general. In Britain, his friendship with the Royal Family is well known—especially his racing companionship with Prince Philip and more recently, Prince Charles, aboard the Fox-designed Flying Fifteen *Coweslip*. Also well-known in Britain (resulting in a C.B.E.) was his design of the self-bailing, self-righting Airborne Lifeboat which could be launched from rescue aircraft. Powered and fueled for a thousand miles, with sufficient food for a month, the boat was capable of carrying twenty-five men in any sea. It is credited with saving the lives of many airmen—but could also have been used to rescue warship crews in major battles.

"I have designed many boats in my life that I have been proud of; but nothing has given me such deep and lasting joy and contentment as the fact that I was . . . able to design these Airborne Lifeboats which saved so many brave airmen's lives. Possibly I may never be in the position to do such a satisfying job again. Even if it is so, I am well content. I gave of my best and the result came up to all the hopes and expectations that I, always an optimist, held."

Uffa Fox

In this country, Uffa Fox's influence has been less obvious, but just as seminal. His desire to outwit the sea led to the development of planing sailboats; his first, *Avenger*, began racing in 1928 and with Fox at the helm, piled up an amazing record of fifty-two firsts, two seconds, and three thirds in fifty-seven starts during her first racing season. More work on planing hulls came before and during the war, culminating in the "Flying Family," of which the Flying Fifteen is the best-known here. The Albacore, of which there are a few hundred in this country, is a 15-foot Uffa Fox one-design planing dinghy aimed at family racing. Fox is also credited with the 12-foot Firefly, a one-time Olympic class that has been superseded by the Finn. But probably the most popular of his boats is the O'Day Day Sailer. Legend has it that the boat was sketched out at a meeting during the 1958 London Boat Show between Fox and George O'Day; Fox says, "It is one of the most pleasing boats I have yet designed." Obviously many Americans feel the same way; there are some five thousand of the ubiquitous 17-foot Day Sailers in the United States.

Not the least of Uffa Fox's contributions has been his influence on powerboat design—in particular, high-speed offshore hydroplaning craft. His lifelong study of hulls—ones that are fast, seaworthy, and plane yet remain in contact with the water—began with his apprenticeship to the S.E. Saunders firm in England before World War I during which he helped design and build *Maple Leaf IV*. It was the first boat to achieve a speed of 50 knots and won the Harmsworth Trophy in 1912-13, "defeating the Americans and all the world." *Anglesy* (*I* and *II*), and Sir Max Aitken's *Black Maria* (designed for the Cowes-Torquay race of 1963) are the most famous of Fox's post-war attempts to develop a boat that would plane level at high speeds without trim tabs. His warnings against constant deadrise (rise of floor from amidships aft) which causes porpoising at high speeds and, he claims, contributed to the death of Donald Campbell in *Bluebird*, are now part of the literature and state of the art.

Also part of the literature are five books, written before the war and now classics, on sailing, seamanship, yacht design, and construction. Since the war, *Seamanlike Sense in Powercraft*, published in England in 1968, and just recently in the United States (Henry Regnery Co.) analyzes classic powerboats to illustrate designed-in seaworthiness. *Handling Sailing Boats According to Uffa* (Newnes, London) is now about twelve years old, but is full of common sense about basic sailing, racing, and cruising. Sandwiched between his more technical texts are memoirs like *More Joys of Living* (sequel to *Joys of Living*) published this year (Nautical House, London), which celebrate one man's life as a seafarer, designer, musician, racing sailor, singer of sea chanteys, and consummate storyteller. His works are full of little homiletics on things like bad weather ("Do not put to sea as you will get all you want of it without deliberately going out in it"), seasickness ("If I am in charge of a vessel I always have boiled fowls, enough to last for the first forty-eight hours at sea"), cooking fish ("We should always use a fish kettle the same size as the fish itself") and rest ("Never stand when we can sit; never sit when we can lie"). Uffa's Ten Commandments on leading the good physical life run the gamut from advice on avoiding constipation to tips on sensible drinking.

Homilies aside, several generations of small-boat sailors have grown up on Uffa Fox's books, and they are well worth reading. There is a great deal of wisdom in his writing about the sea coupled with a puckish sense of humor and a reverence for the natural world.

All of this filters through when you meet him. Uffa Fox is indeed alive and living in Cowes on the Isle of Wight, but at 74, he is not terribly well; a heart ailment limits his activity ("I live on 14 pills a day"). In effect, the immensely strong body that served him well for so many years (he swam in the ocean daily until a few years ago) has deserted him, but his mind is as alert as ever. There is no significant reduction in output; he is still designing, although the drafting chores are left for others. His correspondence with friends all over the world continues voluminously. His love of travel, especially to France, where his wife Yvonne was born, has had to be curtailed. Now he spends his days at the Commodore's House at the harbor's edge in Cowes, and his friends come to see him or check up on him by phone.

Uffa Fox is probably the Isle of Wight's most famous resident, which is not surprising since he was born and spent a good deal of his professional life there and is, in fact, named after an ancient king of the area. The island, across the Solent from Southampton, figures in much of his writing:

"I tried twice to live in America, but although I loved its people because of their great kindness and hospitality, I missed all the history and romance of Europe . . . we Islanders are fortunate as all around us are sites of ancient British encampments, remains of Roman villas and medieval castles all of which add delight and romance to our lives."

Close to mainland England, yet close to the sea as well, lying as it does between the English Channel and the coast, the Isle of Wight breeds seafarers, as one begins to understand in traveling there. I had taken an early train down from London, feasted superbly enroute, and arrived in Southampton in time to catch a Hovercraft to Cowes, some forty minutes across the Solent. This neck of water, with its strong tides and currents, yet sheltered from the open Channel by the island, is one of the traditional spawning grounds of British yachtsmen, and Cowes, with its narrow cobbled streets and ship chandleries, reflects this kinship. Not knowing where Uffa Fox lived, I simply asked a storekeeper and was directed to Hewitt's Grocery, behind which Uffa's house—a 400-year-old restored warehouse—sits on its own wharf overlooking the water.

"The perfect place for me was a rambling, great, disused and ancient warehouse with the sea washing three sides of it, at whose quay in the old days, brigs and other sailing vessels lay along side to discharge and take aboard their cargoes."

Uffa Fox

This, after an enormous amount of redesigning and rebuilding, the addition of balconies and central heating, a giant kitchen, bedrooms, dining-living room, and the like, became his headquarters—the Commodore's House.

The second floor—with its dining-salon area, kitchen, and drafting room—is where we spent the better part of the day talking. There were interruptions: the vicar called with news about a fire in his church the night before and received a tot of scotch and a pound note for his collection box; the clockman came and went after winding the collection of ship's clocks; there was lunch of a chop and glass of ale, and best of all, Uffa's comments about the vista of the Solent before us. Constantly alert to the wind changes and the coming and going of the craft in the harbor, he also had his eyes on the international fleet of Dragons racing for the Duke of Edinburgh Cup and commented irreverently on three dismastings that took place during the course of the regatta. This irreverence, never sarcastic, but with good humor, is as much a part of the Uffa Fox style as the great collection of stories and sea chanteys with which he is wont to entertain visitors. We had some of those, too, accompanied by laughter and a wagging of the expressive eyebrows that are an Uffa Fox trademark.

Near the end of our time together, I asked him what advice he would give to a young designer. "Well," he said, "he wouldn't earn a lot of money but he would have a most wonderful life because he would meet all the best people on earth. When you go sailing, you have to put up with whatever the Lord sends.

"Look at those Dragons out there. It's blowing quite hard and they're battling and having a rough time and they're wet through and cold. But if a man puts up with that, he's a good fellow. So this young designer, he will meet the salt of the earth. And he will have fun.

"I'm seventy-four now—got this bad heart. I can't walk upstairs—got to have a lift [elevator]. I've got to have a bosun's chair to lift me in and out of my boats, but I enjoy life now more than ever before. I've balanced everything up. Because once you're seventy, that's the end of your days. I've already had four years extra, and every day is full of fun."

* * *

"Many times in my life I have narrowly missed sudden death and have often been very close to it in peace and war. Sailing the Atlantic in little boats has brought the fear of death to me many times, but on these occasions there is so much movement and action that there is little place for fear in our hearts.

"And now I have learned that a quiet departure from earth is also not a thing to dread, that when it is time for mine, as I already have the sea flowing in my veins, I have only to be clothed by the heavens and crowned with light to be complete and able to enjoy Paradise.

"So when death's dark angel glides silently invisible alongside, to bear my innermost spirit aloft, I shall go happily and not flinch."

Uffa Fox

4

Eighty-Five Years of Boating as Seen in Rudder

Proper Yachting Dress

FEBRUARY, 1891

There are social usages in this world which a great many of us are apt to slight. This is especially so with the yachtsman. How often have we seen the gilded ball-room youth in togs that would disgrace his butler when afloat. It is a pernicious habit this putting on of overalls and rags when you go yachting. Remember that you have your social duties to perform afloat, and a man should always appear in proper togs when lying in a harbor or sailing about a resort that is populated with people of refinement and good breeding. This article will treat only of the small boat owner, and we will assume he has a crew of four, to wit: the master, the quartermaster and two seamen. The yacht owner's uniform for social dress should be a double-breasted blue reefer, closing with black buttons. This wearing of brass and bouilion is *passe* and the well-dressed yachtsman of today wears all his ornamentation upon his cap. The trousers should be of blue, or of white flannel, while the cap may be of the same colors. The blue yachting cap, however, should be the hat worn with social dress. In this suit the shirt should be a linen one, with starched bosom, collars and cuffs; and you should be careful to appear as clean and gentlemanly as the limited boudoir arrangements of your boat will permit. The generally accepted marks or insignia for a boat owner is two fouled anchors on the cap; a non-boat owner wears one fouled anchor, and flag officers are known by silver stars above the anchors. The working dress of the yachtsman is a different affair. The most sensible is a white jersey or sweater over it, white duck trousers and white canvas rubber-soled shoes. The rig is comfortable, durable and looks neat.

For evening hops and receptions ashore the regular full-dress suit generally worn on such occasions is the only proper dress, though yachtsmen with small boats may be excused for appearing in the dress described in the first part of this article. The full dress suit for yachtsmen is made of blue cloth and is ornamented with brass buttons. The uniforming of a crew is a matter that few yachtsmen give the proper attention to. The man before the mast should have three outfits, to wit: his blues or dress, his whites or fatigues, and his oilers. The regulation yachting crew's uniform is of blue, the shirt of flannel, ornamented with white braid around the collar, and the yacht's name in white on the breast, a white cord lanyard, blue man-o'-war trousers and pancake hat, black silk scarf. The working dress is generally a blue Guernsey, white canvas trousers, worsted watch cap and canvas shoes with rubber soles. The master's uniform is of blue flannel, cap, coat and trousers. The master wears upon his right arm, between the elbow and shoulder, a silver fouled anchor. The engineer wears a Maltese cross; the assistant engineer a three-bladed propeller wheel; the boatswain a spread eagle; the quartermaster a pair of binocular glasses, and the coxswain a pair of oars crossed. In the small boats, and especially on race days, the amateur crews should all dress alike. There is no sight so pretty as a properly and uniformly dressed crew, working a boat in a thrashing good wind.

Progress

by *Thomas Fleming Day*

MAY, 1900

The ladder by which we are passing from sail to power is what is known as the auxiliary. By means of this the sail-user works his way down from canvas to screw without too roughly jarring his desires or prejudices. With one hand he clings to the sail; with the other he grasps the engine. "I will not give up the sail," he cries. "I will keep it and have the engine likewise." He does! For how long? Until he finds out that it is an unsatisfactory combination. I have many times explained why this is so. As a substitute for power, sail has a value; as a substitute for sail, power is also of use. But as auxiliaries, they are both failures. Let a man put into a boat an engine that will drive her at an equal or greater speed than her speed under canvas, and he will not employ the latter. After the first season's experience, he will discard the sail; it is expensive, and the aid it gives is not worth the labor it takes to set it. How many of our auxiliaries constantly use their sails for sailing? Very few. You can go to windward quicker with the engine than you can beat-up. You go to leeward or reach faster with the engine than you can under canvas, unless it is blowing a strong breeze. How often does such a breeze blow in our sailing season? One day out of three? No, not one day out of six.

I met a man last summer in a yawl-rigged auxiliary. He had unbent his mainsail. "It was in the way of the awning," he explained. "I can do all the sailing I have to under jib and jigger." I suggested a change in the rig that would make the boat what it should have been in the first place—a craft with steadying canvas only. What is the use of putting gaff-headed sails and a lot of top hamper on such boats? Give them a jib-headed trysail and a couple of staysails that can be easily hoisted, lowered, and stowed. The most useful sail for these power boats is a small square sail; going down the wind in a following sea, it will steady-up and prevent rolling. The more boom mainsail you have, the worse power boats will roll when running.

Now, don't go throwing your hands up in the air and exclaiming that I am opposed to the power boat. I am not, nor would it matter if I was. There are thousands of men who delight in them and find health and recreation driving the waters by their aid. Nine-tenths of these men would not come into yachting if they had to use sail craft. They would stay on land and play golf or some other old-woman's game. It is better to have them out in anything rather than not at all. No man can spend his play days on the water and not be better for it.

But while I do not oppose modern innovations that go to make voyaging more comfortable, more safe, and more speedy, I never go into hysterics over them. I wouldn't give a button to cross the Atlantic in four days or ride on an express at the rate of a mile a minute. I have never made a god of speed nor knelt at the shrine of any of the deities of modern civilization. There is a lot of tommyrot talked about the thing we call *progress*. The world would be better off if it went ahead at half the rate it does. We would get there just the same and have a lot of breath to spare. As it is, when we reach the goal, we have only enough left in our lungs to give one cheer and then drop.

The Remarkable New Wave

OCTOBER, 1907

The first actual application of radio telephony to practical work anywhere in the world was made at Put-in-Bay, on Lake Erie, during the
week of July 15th-20th, in reporting the regatta of the Interlake Association. The Radio Telephone Company installed the DeForest wireless
telephone on board the cruiser yacht *Thelma*, owned by Commodore
W. R. Huntington, of Elyria, Ohio, and also equipped a shore station at
the Fox Dock at Put-in-Bay. *Thelma* is thus the first craft in the world to
be fully equipped with the wireless phone, an honor which it is fair to say
will make it historic in coming years.

Although not well-suited to the task, on account of her short spars
and wooden hull, *Thelma* gave a most excellent account of herself by
the Radio 'phone throughout the entire regatta. The distances which
were attained exceeded the hopes of Dr. Lee DeForest, the inventor,
who was in charge of the apparatus. *Thelma* followed the competing
yachts around the course through most of the races, and full and graphic
accounts were telephoned into the shore station, exactly as the events
occurred. Speech alone was not transmitted during these convincing
demonstrations, but singing, whistling, and gramophone music or
dialogues were interpolated with the news reports.

The greatest distance at which the reports from the yachts were heard and recorded was four miles, considered remarkable in view of the height of *Thelma*'s spars and the power of the transmitter on board. Her equipment comprised a 220-volt generator of one-kilowatt capacity, the DeForest oscillator and transmitter, and for the receiving apparatus an Audion detector and "pancake" form of syntonizer or tuner. Her aerial wires led through the roof of the wheel house to a small crossarm on top of the foremast and thence to a smaller arm on the mainmast. Ground connection was at first made to the propeller shafts of her twin screws, but as this was found insufficient, more area was added by fastening two sheets of zinc to the yacht's hull at the bow.

Thelma is a trim little cruiser yacht of 17.82 tons net, length over all 72 feet, with a 10-foot-8 breadth and 5-foot draught. She carries two 20-horsepower Lacy engines and is schooner-rigged. The telephone dynamo was belted direct to the flywheel of her starboard engine, aft, and the rest of the Radio apparatus was mounted on a small table in her main cabin, convenient to all.

As a sample of the service which the DeForest Radio 'phone performed during the Put-in-Bay regatta, the following synopsis of the report of the morning races of Friday, July 19th, will be of interest. The man in charge of the shore station, not being a stenographer, it was possible for him to write down only the first words of a conversation, or brief headings of the reports. This illustrates incidentally the great advantage in point of expedition of business of the Radio telephone over the wireless telegraph. From three to four times the number of words can be transmitted in a given length of time.

"9:57½ a.m. I will tell you when the first boat crosses the line. First boat is about crossing the line—9:59. *Spray* crossed the line—9:59. *Spray* crossed about 25 seconds after 9:59; 9:59:05 is the exact time." Later: "Second boat just crossed—10:07½. First in the catboat race crossed at 10:01½. *Cleveland* finished second; time 10:03½; *Borealis* 10:04¼. *Cleveland* finished second. What shall I put down for you in the second race? *St. Clair* just crossed 10:07½ [repeated often]. Hello, Frank. We will be back in about two hours. *Osekita* just crossed the line. You spell it; I can't. Time 10:08½," etc., until the races were finished and *Thelma* started back for Put-in-Bay dock.

Upon the finish of the regatta the telephone apparatus from *Thelma* and the Put-in-Bay shore station was shipped to Toledo, where it is the intention of the Radio Telephone Company to install it permanently, where it can be in communication with other wireless 'phone sets to be installed on vessels sailing Lake Erie. The Great Lakes offer, perhaps, the most promising field anywhere in the world for the first general application of this new invention to the needs of a merchant marine, and it is the intention of the company to at once enter this promising field.

How to Fly

by William Harper, Jr.

FEBRUARY, 1910

"The aeroplane," wrote Harper, "is the natural evolution of the sailing yacht; in fact, it is the yacht of the sky." So Harper and Rudder *thought it logical to tell readers how to build and fly a little two-passenger biplane. With remarkable economy of page space, Harper describes how to build the biplane in the first 2,800 words of his article. The remaining 600 words, excerpted here, tell how to get it off the ground.*

This aeroplane, while it will go 40 miles per hour at sea level, may go 80 miles at a 10,000-foot altitude, the propeller rotating proportionally faster but not consuming any more power. For this reason, it is probable that we shall soon have aeroplanes making long flights at the rate of 100 miles per hour with as much safety as we now travel "The Briny Deep."

As it is the purpose of this article not to delve into the probable, but to disclose the construction of a practical air craft, I will endeavor to give some general instructions as to its operation and what one may expect to negotiate while learning to sail it.

First, the flight is started by a run of about 100 yards on some smooth track of ground where there is no obstruction for about 1,000 feet ahead.

After everything is made ready and the operator well braced in his seat, the engine is started by giving the propeller a cranking turn, and the machine moves forward on its wheels.

The speed of travel increases at every turn of the 10-foot propeller and just as soon as one feels that he is going at a rate of over 20 miles per hour he pulls back the lever operating the forward plane or vertical rudder (which has, to begin with, been kept pitched down, holding the aeroplane to the ground), elevating it, and the whole machine is instantly pointed upward so gently that at first you do not realize that you have left the earth.

The first flights should be made slowly at about 6 feet from the ground until one is accustomed to the swaying movement. However, it is not unlike that of a graceful boat, only you seem to be rushing through space like an express train.

After you are sure of yourself and the machine, it is better to keep well up, as the most accidents are caused by collisions with trees or not being sufficiently above the ground to right yourself when being tossed about a little.

For this reason a yachtsman will certainly make a better aeronaut than a "landlubber." The whole thing is to adapt yourself to the motion of the machine.

While in the air, the management of the aeroplane is very similar to that of a yacht, and every good sailor will find it almost second nature to keep his machine under proper headway.

When rounding a curve, the pendulum will raise the outer plane [wing] tip, making the machine keel over so to speak, thereby restoring equilibrium to the machine and not allowing it to skid.

It is not necessary to run the engine at its full speed all the time, but it is advisable after ascending to any altitude to slow it down as much as possible and practice soaring, always, however, keeping under sufficient headway to make the balancing planes effective.

By this you will discover that while the engine is required to develop all its power to raise the machine off the ground, it requires but a small porportion of that power to sustain the flight once under proper headway.

The descent is made by depressing the forward plane and bringing the machine close to the ground with a smooth, open stretch of 100 yards ahead, and descending, after having stopped the engine, at a very acute angle, at the same time applying the brakes to the wheels.

As the machine touches the surface with no weight until its momentum is diminished, there is no appreciable shock.

Voyage into War

by Colonel Duncan F.D. Neill

SEPTEMBER, 1914

The voyage of the 1914 cup challenger began well. A gale in Falmouth, England, had ended, and sun shown on Sir Thomas Lipton's Shamrock IV *and her tender, the yacht* Erin, *as they left harbor. Lipton had grown wealthy by applying P.T. Barnum showmanship to the grocery business; hundreds of his stores spread throughout Britain. His luck hadn't extended to his sportsmanlike attempts at wresting away the cup, however. Three previous challenges going back to 1898 had been lost. But as the voyage began on July 21, 1914, hopes were high.* Shamrock, *under the command of Colonel Neill, carried 2,000 square feet more sail than the American defender,* Resolute. *Lipton's boat had been designed by Charles E. Nicholson, sometimes called the Herreshoff of England, to be sturdy and fast.*

Within three weeks, the contest for the cup had become irrelevant.

The Coast Guard station and lighthouse on the headland signaled us a pleasant passage, always a cheerful message blown from the flagstaff to the sailor about to start on his long voyage with uncertainties ahead.

Shamrock set her big square sail for the first time this morning, and it did good service as the wind was right aft; the tide was helping us as it ran to the westward and soon the Lizard Light was abeam. The signal station on Lizard Head wished us success, and it seemed when we answered this, that that was our last message from home; but not so, as Lord Inverclyde came along in his steam yacht *Beryl* bound home to the Clyde, and passing close under our stern, he shouted out his best wishes, and his flags signaled the old wish again. The wind by this time, noon, had dropped, and *Shamrock* lay in a glassy calm ten miles south of Lizard, rolling about in the long swell caused by the heavy sea of yesterday. We aboard *Erin* decided to take the challenger in tow, as the tide by now had turned, and we were being carried back toward Falmouth, so we passed the hawser on board *Shamrock* and towed her along at about 9 knots. Towards midnight a light northerly breeze sprang up, so we cast off the *Shamrock*. Soon the breeze increased, and at eight bells in the morning watch she was sailing along at a good 9 knots, rolling about a bit in the swell, but shipping no water. Except for a little spray splashing to windward from her long flat bow, she seemed wonderfully dry.

The glass kept rising all through the night, and we were in the best of spirits, for we had hopes of a fair wind for some time to come, and the 22nd of July found us rolling across the bay, and going strong. At noon the sky was too overcast to get sights, but the log gave us 247 miles as the day's run. The ship was rolling about a lot in the swell, and this proved very trying for the gear, but everything likely to get chafed was carefully parcelled with canvas.

In the bay we passed a French fishing boat trailing for bonito. Sticking out on either side were long poles to which were attached several lines with hooks, somewhat resembling the mackerel-whiffers of Plymouth Sound on a big scale. These fishermen go a long way out from port in pursuit of their arduous calling. Fishermen at sea always appeal to me, as it is there one sees them at their best. The deep-sea steam trawler has a tender place in our hearts as we see him diving into big seas, dragging the banks for the food of us landsmen. How few of us who complain that our fish is not quite fresh for breakfast think of what it has cost the men to get it to our tables.

Gradually she dips below the horizon to the northward and we are again alone on the big ocean, this little fleet of Sir Thomas Lipton's. We are really not away from the world, as we used to be when out on the ocean on former voyages, for we have the wonderful invention of Marconi to keep us in touch with our friends. As the *Erin* has one of the finest installations afloat, we are well supplied with news by Sir Thomas, who is always anxious to help us, and we exchange messages daily.

July 27th—A beautiful day, but calm. Early this morning we sighted land right ahead, the Island of Terceira, and gradually it came up over the horizon as we drew slowly nearer, being piloted in by the sea swallows which came out to greet us. The afternoon became flat calm, and after drifting about on the glassy sea for several hours we had to get *Shamrock* in tow, as the current was setting her back fast. It is a great pity this having to tow, as she looks so beautiful sailing along. We let her sail as much as possible, only taking her in tow when she is at a standstill.

Late in the afternoon we were abreast of the island, which looked lovely and green with little white villages down by the water's edge— such a contrast to us who had seen nothing but the big blue ocean for so long.

These islands of the Azores are of volcanic origin, and one sees the volcanic nature of the soil when passing close to the cliffs. The sunset tonight was gorgeous, the pink rays of the afterglow striking up across the pale blue of the sky. These pale pink rays shot up across the western dome like spokes of some great fiery wheel. Let us hope it is the wheel of fortune turning for us.

We passed through between the islands during the night, and anchored inside Fayal breakwater at 7 a.m. on Tuesday morning, July 28th, having covered 1,255 miles in 7 days 3 hours, an average speed of 7.3 knots. We went on board the *Shamrock* and found all well, and transferred the crew we had aboard the *Erin* to the racer. The *Erin* coaled all day, and aboard the *Shamrock* all were busy making light-weather sails out of some old *Shamrock III* sails we had taken with us on the *Erin*, as we are determined to get her along better in the calms. We spent the day here in the quiet little harbor, all oblivious to the wars and rumors of wars we hear are disturbing the minds of Europe; and we hope to resume our voyage westward tonight or early in the morning.

July 29th—Up early to find a beautiful morning, we got under way shortly after 5 a.m. and steamed around the western end of Fayal Island. Wind very light, so we took *Shamrock* in tow to get an offing. The island looked pretty in the morning light as it gradually brightened up, and one could see the light smoke from the cottages, showing signs of the waking inhabitants. By six o'clock a light northwesterly breeze sprang up, so we let go *Shamrock*. The breeze gradually increased, and during the forenoon it was blowing fresh, letting the challenger slip along at a good pace on the port tack. There was still a long northwesterly swell, which increased considerably as the day advanced, making it very uncomfortable for the sailing vessel, which pitched about a lot in the head sea. To make matters worse, the glass inclined to fall, so sail was reduced, and as the night wore on matters got worse and *Shamrock* could make very little of it, being more or less hove-to during the dark watches.

The morning of the 30th was none too good, the sea and weather conditions being very much the same as yesterday, *Shamrock* still going along slowly on port tack under reduced canvas. The day was very cloudy, with threatening rain, but the weather cleared towards noon, and the wind went westerly. *Shamrock* tacked a few times, and we seemed to be sailing round Corvo Island some 10 to 12 miles off. Towards afternoon, the wind shifted to the north of west, letting *Shamrock* lay a better course. In addition to the change of wind for the better, the sea moderated a lot. The glass still inclined to fall and the night looked threatening, so prudence made it advisable to reef the mainsail and stow the mizzen and staysail and take in the topsail. It was well these precautions were taken, because during the middle watch, on the morning of the 31st, there came tearing down from the W.N.W. a very heavy squall with a deluge of rain. *Shamrock* tore through it at great speed and logged 12 knots for the ensuing hour, and continued at 11 knots for quite a while, as long as the strong wind lasted. A very heavy swell pooped her and put out the tail lamp on the taffrail.

August 4th—E.S.E. breeze, light but fair, square sail set, less rolling. *Shamrock* kept sailing all afternoon, gradually going slower. Towards sunset we spoke a fair-sized barque, slowly sailing, or rather drifting, to the southward, close-hauled in the light air, and the *Erin* steamed close alongside of her. In response to our ensign being hoisted on the flagstaff, she showed Italian colors, and dipped bunting with us in greeting and farewell. She was the *Rosan* of Genoa, bound for Rosario with a cargo of wood. One of her seamen shouted over to us, "Good luck to the *Shamrock*!"—evidently some hard-up British sailor who had been forced by circumstances to ship before the mast on a foreign vessel. One of the waifs or strays of the seafaring world. Paid off from one vessel, they go ashore with their hard-earned wages in pocket, and go on a spree until all their money is gone. The "sharks" and "harpies" get the better of them, and in a day or two they are forced to take any job they can get. Good, true men they are at heart, as this greeting to the *Shamrock* showed. These are the tragedies of the sea one hears nothing of. With a farewell salute of the ensign we parted, and the *Erin* steamed over towards the *Shamrock* again. In half an hour's time or so the wind failed her altogether so that she barely had steerageway, so we decided to pass her the towline. As it was dark by this time we had to fix a Holmes light onto the buoy at the end of the hauling line, and with the help of the light spluttering in the water they managed to get hold of the rope and got the wire aboard. Then we started off on our course westward again.

Tonight we heard by wireless that the British government had decided to go to war with Germany. Only a few words reached us, but what significance they conveyed! To think that we were to be at war with a first-class European power! We could hardly realize it, and everybody was dismayed and downhearted at the awful prospect. For token of the terrible catastrophe impending Europe, the sun rose on the morning of August 5th in anger. It seemed as if the eastern sky was bathed in blood, so red and fiery it was.

As the day lengthened, the sea became flat calm. Nothing disturbed the surface of the sea but the flying-fish. Our distance at noon was 146 miles. In the afternoon, seeing it was so calm, we decided to stop and change the crew on *Shamrock* and sent over fresh water and provisions. This was a much easier matter today than on the last occasion, as there was practically no swell, so we got on board the challenger and had a good inspection of her above and below. We found everything in first-class order. She was not in such fine trim as when she left Gosport, but we had much to be thankful for, as in reality we had not had any bad weather. The ocean so far has been very kind to the four-leaved *Shamrock*, which is a sign that she is sailing under a lucky star. Three or four trips between *Erin* and *Shamrock* sufficed to get the men changed and all the water and stores aboard, and getting back to the *Erin* we resumed the voyage. What a perfect afternoon and evening it was. No war here; all was gentle and peaceful.

As one looks on the vast ocean and sees the heavens lit up in all their glory, one cannot realize that passion and hate are loose on the land. Surely we are going to a land of quiet and content, for the sun sinks in all its splendor down below the western horizon, as it were into a land of peace. Let us hope that President Wilson's message for peace will prevail with those in council in Europe. Tonight the moon shone red from the eastern horizon, as if she had just risen drenched in blood—a bad omen, we thought.

August 6th—Dawn came in cold and grey, with rain squalls brooding. We started the oil wave-subduer from the *Erin* and steamed ahead of *Shamrock*, which helped her a lot. We were instructed by a wireless message to tow her the rest of the way into New York, if necessary, on account of the war; but it was impossible to tow in such a sea, so the challenger had to continue on her own sailing as best she could.

About eight o'clock on the morning of the 7th, *Shamrock* wore ship and went off on starboard tack, steering S. 50 W. There was too much head sea on for her to tack round. Several very heavy rain squalls passed over the vessel in the morning, and the wind still blew fresh from W. by N. The day was bright and very hot, but it was not until 7 p.m. that we were able to get the hawser on board *Shamrock*, as the sea had not moderated enough until then; and even then we had to steam dead slow, about 4 or 5 knots at most, in order not to strain the racer, which rolled and pitched about at the end of the towline as we headed into the wind on our straight course for New York. After going along for some time at this pace, we got a signal from *Shamrock* by flash lamp to go slower and use oil to try and kill the head swell, so we reduced the speed of the engines until they were barely turning, and we set the oiler going, which considerably reduced the waves in our wake. At 10 p.m. we received this message by wireless:

"Capt. Pascoe, S. Y. Erin. *Proceed to nearest friendly port."*

We decided to make for Bermuda, 450 miles away, as it was the nearest and, we thought, the safest place to make for, being out of the track of shipping. Halifax, the next nearest British port, was 480 miles, but right across the track of shipping, and we had heard that there were a couple of German cruisers in the vicinity. One, the *Dresden*, kept getting and sending messages in code all the time. We altered course, and getting the swell more abeam, managed to make better progress.

August 8th—A very fine day, and extremely hot; light wind on starboard bow, just enough to cool the air on the weather side. Splendid night; *Shamrock* going well, but a little rolling after midnight. Received the above message from Sayville shore station, but we did not answer, as we had decided not to send any message out which might reveal our whereabouts. In any case we could not get in touch with the shore as we were too far off, although we could hear the powerful shore stations quite well. It is a wonderful invention, the wireless telegraph, and certainly it has helped us. Without it we would have been sailing calmly along towards New York, quite oblivious of the war going on, and might have sailed into the jaws of the *Dresden* and been captured. Who knows?

August 9th—The best day; quite a calm day with a gentle northerly air. We managed to make good speed. Today at 11 a.m. we got a wireless from *H.M.S. Suffolk*, one of the British cruisers rounding up the Germans, asking what ship we were. Answered and hoisted our ensign on both vessels. Shortly after this we intercepted a message from the German cruiser *Dresden*, which did not seem very far away owing to the strength of the ticking on the receivers. She was telling a German merchantman that a British cruiser was in the offing. We hastened on at as great a speed as we safely could tow *Shamrock*, and with the help of her sails, set when a little breeze came on forward of the beam on south side, we managed to do 11 knots and sighted the lighthouse of Bermuda about 5:30. We quickly brought the island up and got the boarding officer on board just as the sun was setting. The island being under military law, the boarding officer came aboard first and when he had satisfied himself that we were all right, he went off to his vessel and sent a pilot on board to take us into an anchorage for the night, while the boarding officer towed *Shamrock* in with his tug. The pilot gave us newspapers in which we read news of the war, all horrible enough, but we must go through with it now. It is not of our making; we must and will defend our rights at all costs, however terrible it may be. The searchlights ashore are sweeping the horizon incessantly all night, and we feel safe and thankful to be here under the protection of our own flag.

August 10th—The pilot remained on board all last night and early in the morning the medical officer came on board and gave us practique, so we got under way for Hamilton. *Shamrock* was towed out of the snug harbor of St. George by the boarding officer's boat, and tied on behind *Erin*; we towed her through the intricate channel between the coral reefs.

It was a lovely day, and interesting to us as we saw the island for the first time. Opposite the Naval Station at Ireland Island, we go into the inland sea through a narrow channel, dredged out of the coral just like a canal with water on each bank as it were. Here we passed and saluted two French cruisers—one the *Conde*—who were coaling, getting ready to help in the rounding up of the Germans. We entered the pretty inland sea and steamed between the little wooded islands with nice summer dwellings on them; to us they looked like summer residences, but in these beautiful islands it is always summer. We had a great reception steaming into Hamilton, being cheered by the populace and the American visitors, also the crews of the two mailboats which were hung up here owing to the war. Marshal law was proclaimed in the islands, and one sees on all hands signs of war preparations. We called at Government House and on the Port Captain, as the Admiral was out at sea on one of the cruisers pursuing the German ships. The Captain of the Port told us we would have to leave our naval reservists here, so we made arrangements to transfer them.

August 11th—Very hot day; waiting instructions to proceed. Today we received a very fine telegram from Sir Thomas, congratulating Captains Pascoe and Turner and their officers and men on the pluck they had shown in bringing the yachts safely to this British port. All hands gave three cheers for the generous owner, when they heard he had let all their families know by telegram of the safe arrival of the crews and ships. The day was spent pleasantly sailing about in the cutters and dodging the sun under awnings.

August 12th—This day reminds us of many pleasant days spent on the moors at home among the heather, for is this not the day for grouse shooting to commence? How many of our sportsmen will have fired at their last grouse ere the 12th comes round again?

We lunched at the Royal Bermuda Yacht Club with Commodore Gosling and spent a most enjoyable time, thanks to the kindness and hospitality of the genial commodore and his fellow-members.

August 13th—Again exceedingly hot, bathing being the chief and most popular amusement, as the water in the harbor was 86 degrees. We left Hamilton at 2 p.m. and Captain Brown, R.N., captain in charge of the dockyard, came on board and we handed over to him the reservists, five from *Erin* and four from *Shamrock*. The men were sorry to leave their messmates, as we were to lose them, but they went away cheerfully, knowing that they were doing their bit for the service of our Empire, and we wished them luck and gave them three hearty cheers as they steamed off in the dockyard launch. We cleared from Ireland Island at 4 p.m. and shortly afterwards passed through a heavy rain cloud, which must have done good to those on shore who were fortunate to have their land and houses in its path, for these islands depend almost entirely on rain for their water supply, all the houses having cemented roofs to catch the precious liquid.

We dropped the pilot into the patrol vessel, off St. George, and set our course seawards at 5:30 p.m. The night was quite calm, so we steamed along well. What a lovely night, and to think that all Europe is ablaze with fire and sword.

August 14th—Light W. by N. breeze, choppy sea, very warm and muggy. As we are approaching the Gulf Stream, more evident by the heavy rain squalls and choppy sea, we had to alter the course more northerly to shoulder the heavy swell as there was not enough wind to sail *Shamrock* at any speed, and we must get over in case an enemy's cruiser comes up from below the horizon anywhere. The night was calm, but more sea, with much lighting up the northern horizon.

August 15th—Very muggy weather. We are fairly in the Gulf Stream now. Strong westerly breeze, all morning tearing the tops off the sea in whitecaps, *Shamrock* diving into the choppy sea, sending showers of spray over her decks and drenching the men clad in their oilskins. By noon it was so bad that we had to let the *Shamrock* go, and she dodged along under storm canvas, making as good a go of it as she could in the confused sea that rose up on either side like a boiling pot. To windward there was a black squall brewing, which came tearing down on us shortly, accompanied by vivid lightning and thunder, and very heavy rain, so thick that for quite a while we lost sight of the sailing vessel; but of course we knew her whereabouts, and kept the whistle sounding every few minutes to let her know our whereabouts. After some time the rain lessened a little and we made her out sailing along half a mile to leeward of us. Then again she was blotted out. In time the squall cleared off, only to be followed by another almost as severe; but the heavy rain was killing the sea, and as the afternoon wore on the wind dropped, so much so that at eight bells we were able to take her in tow again with practically no wind and very little sea. Such is the weather in the Gulf Stream—hot, muggy, and treacherous. During the height of the sea we kept the oil wave-subduer on and gave *Shamrock* the benefit of less crested waves, for the oil certainly makes a big difference to leeward. The night was very dark, owing to a haze and heavy clouds, but it was lit up by continuous lightning flashes. Although there continued to be little or no wind, there was a new swell coming up from the southwest, which gave promise of the true wind from that direction.

Sunday morning, August 16th, found us across the Stream, steaming at about 8 knots over a calm sea. All afternoon we steamed along in a flat calm, over a glassy sea, and had lots of time to study the sea on and below its surface. We noticed three large whales going along in line ahead like battle cruisers, but peaceful ones, as they moved along with an easy gait. Not so the horrible-looking hammerheaded sharks we saw creeping close to us, as if they were torpedoes set out in deadly earnest, these scavengers of the sea looking for their prey. Then we would pass a turtle, one of which lay on his back flopping his flippers endeavoring to right himself; probably some wave had overturned him. One passes bits of boats and odd pieces of wood, so we must be nearing shore, and this is the drift from the Hudson River.

A bright, starry night was to be our last on this voyage. At 8:15 p.m. the Navesink Light flashed a welcome to us which we were glad to see, for we knew that the ocean's perils were past and that the broad arm of New York Harbor lay open, stretched before us, glad to take this friendly fleet into its bosom.

Close to the Ambrose Light the pilot boarded us, and we steamed up to Quarantine, where we arrived at 12:30 p.m., Monday, August 17. In the early morning we looked around to see what vessels were anchored in company with us, and saw a large vessel painted with black and red funnels like a Danish liner, which turned out to be the *Laconia* of the Cunard Line, disguised, as she had been followed at sea by one of the enemy. We left the anchorage at 9 a.m., after getting practique, and steamed up to South Brooklyn, following the *Shamrock*, which was being towed up by a tug. Sir Thomas Lipton's fleet got a great reception as we steamed along. Steamers crammed with businessmen going to their offices cheered heartily, and every available steam and motor whistle afloat and ashore within sight saluted the challenger. With the din of the noise and the heartiness of the welcome we passed the wharves, getting a hearty cheer from a Russian liner, but being received with silent disdain by the German liners tied to their wharves. Far better had they sent yachts to do battle with us than let loose the dogs of war, as the race has been postponed until this lamentable war is over, which we pray God may be soon. There is nothing for it but to lay up the challenger, which we commenced to do forthwith, and by night she was almost stripped of her ocean gear and laid up in Shewan & Sons Yard, South Brooklyn.

The U-Boat *vs.* the Barkentine

by Walter Boudreau

DECEMBER, 1944

The author grew up on small sailboats. So it seemed natural during a tour of duty with the Merchant Marine in World War II to request assignment to a large sailing cargo ship. There were still a few around in 1943, and the Angelus *was exactly what Boudreau wanted: a 238-ton barkentine. He left Nova Scotia aboard* Angelus *in March of 1943 with a cargo of barrel staves and paper, bound for Barbados. Two months later, on the way back home, the antique vessel met a Nazi U-boat.*

On the fourteenth day out during the midnight watch, a white light fell slowly from the sky and reclined on the surface of the sea.

Two of us had been chatting with the wheelsman, and we three spotted the light together. We looked in surprise at what we thought to be a meteorite or some other natural phenomenon. Our surprise turned to apprehension as first one and then another light followed the first and floated on the sea.

The man standing watch on the forepeak came running aft, and we all muttered and wondered. Immediately another, another, and another light floated slowly down, and the six lights seemed to extend in a long line off to starboard. When the captain, mate, and men of the other watch were called on deck, they looked in amazement at a semicircle of lights which extended all down the starboard side, around the stern, and well along the port side. To the perplexed captain it must have looked as though we were in some well lighted harbor, but his sanity and his navigation indicated that we were many miles from land. By this time the lights had entirely encircled the ship. We were completely mystified and did not know whether we were amidst a huge convoy or under enemy attack. It was not until a few minutes later that the answer came in a dull drone from far to windward which rapidly grew to a roar as a large bomber flew low over us and dropped a flare which made the deck as bright as day. After that the plane dropped no more flares, but circled continuously throughout the night. All hands stayed on deck speculating. We considered hurricane warnings, subs, and a dozen other things. At dawn the plane, which proved to be a twin-motored American flying boat, passed over at mast height a half dozen times, its blinker asking for identification. We answered with ours and ran up the code flags. The plane signaled O.K. and was off in the direction of Bermuda, almost a hundred miles to westward. We were out fifteen days and, as the *Angelus* had no refrigeration, we were starting to think of fresh meat, milk, fruit, and soda fountains. It showed us plainly the difference of the two worlds of machine and sail, and we aboard the old windjammer, and still truly in the age of Drake and Morgan, found it strange to imagine that the pilot of that plane could easily be sitting down in a restaurant eating steak within a few minutes while we had days of travel ahead.

For hours we wondered why the plane had lighted up the ocean for miles around that night, to make the vessel a sitting duck for any prowling U-boat. We all came to the conclusion that subs had been sighted in that vicinity and that we were for a time suspected of being a mother ship. We decided that the lights which had surrounded us in a tremendous circle had been to trap any U-boat which might have been skulking away. If the pilot of that plane reads this, I hope he will let me know if our guess was right.

During the next four days we bowled along at a great rate into quickly cooling weather. Mackinaws were to be seen on night watches, and there was no more dragging alongside at the end of a short rope.

It was in this kind of weather that we saw the dawn of May 19th. About six o'clock the mate's son Sandy, who was at the wheel, saw something far to leeward. The mate thought it could be either a small patrol boat with a mast or the conning tower of a sub. The captain was called, and a moment's scrutiny with the binoculars confirmed the presence of a submarine. All hands had no sooner come on deck than a shell whined over the bow. Men rushed below for what they could salvage. The captain got the code books in their steel box weighted with lead. Sextants, chronometer, and charts were snatched up. The men gathered oilskins and blankets. The crash of the U-boat's gun spoke again, and all hands rushed to the lifeboat. We had two provisioned dories also, but decided to get away in the lifeboat before it was hit by shell. Ten men and the ship's dog piled into the boat, and we drew away from the vessel as quickly as we could. The sub closed in to two hundred yards now, and all eyes strained to make out the flag fluttering atop the conning tower. Gradually we saw a red flag with a white circle in its center enclosing a black swastika. The captain's hand grasping the weighted steel box containing the code flags had been held over the side; now his hand opened and the box sank into the depths of the ocean.

We agreed that it would be wiser to face the sub than to row off in the other direction and, keeping time carefully to make a good impression, we rowed to within three hundred feet of the Nazis before we noticed that they were training all deck guns on us and loading. We stopped quickly, put up our oars and waited. The diesel engines muttered deeply and the sub went slowly astern until her narrow bow faced us. I had seen a moving picture in which a sub performed this maneuver prior to running down a boat and my imagination began to work. The low-lying craft eased forward, and when the knife-like bow was not many feet away, and our hearts were in our mouths, she veered a bit to starboard and came to a stop. We looked into the business end of a large rapid-fire gun. A machine gun was mounted on a tripod in the conning tower, and we saw young "supermen" putting ammunition clips into it and looking expectantly along the barrel. Another played with the trigger of what looked like a tommy gun. I guess all our imaginations were running riot by this time, but we sat quietly and tried to read the faces of the men looking down at us. Perhaps twenty seconds passed

during which our dog barked furiously and someone tried to quiet him
by twisting hard on his collar.

The Jerry captain, a fellow of no more than 40, broke into a smile.
Without accent, he asked in English, "Who is your captain?"

Captain Jensen stood up and nodded.

"Have you any weapons in your boat?"

"No."

"Come alongside."

We did so and passed a bow and stern line to two young Nazis, each
armed with a revolver.

"Captain, come here."

Captain Jensen leaped to the iron deck and looked up at the man in
the conning tower.

"What is the name of your vessel, captain?"

"*Angelus*."

"Canadian?"

"Yes."

"Where are you bound?"

"To Nova Scotia."

"Halifax?"

"Yes."

"From?"

"Barbados."

"What cargo are you carrying?"

"Molasses."

"Nothing else?"

"No, just molasses."

"Have you any fresh fruit or meat?"

Captain Jensen relayed this question to the cook.

"Naw, but old salt meat, salt fish, potatoes, and yams."

"Are there any instruments or charts aboard the vessel that you
need?" asked the Jerry.

"Well, we could . . ." Captain Jensen began.

"If so, get them within twenty minutes," he said, looking at his
watch, "for after that we are going to shell."

Captain Jensen nodded several times, turned, and came back to the
boat. As he did so we heard the German captain say, "Good luck." This
gesture was spoiled a moment later by a young Nazi handling our lines
who shot up his hand and muttered, "Heil Hitler!"

Casting off, we were not sure what to do. Some were for going back to the vessel, getting our valuables, more food, and taking the two dories in tow. The *Angelus* had drifted off quite a distance by now, and we rowed toward her for a few minutes. Then someone mentioned that it would take at least twenty minutes to get to the vessel and that the shelling might start while we were aboard and hole the boat. The captain was of this opinion and decided that, as we had enough food to keep us alive for as many days as we were likely to be at sea, we had better get away with our whole skins while we had them, before the Nazis had a change of heart.

Putting up the mast with its little red mainsail and jib, we headed north and away from the U-boat.

Immediately the shelling started. The first one went over, the second fell short, and the third took away the foremast. Another blew the galley off the stern. Then the shells began to thud into the hull, and the rapid-fire gun joined in with a clatter. The old barkentine began to smoke. When we left her that morning she had all sail on. Now most of these were burning fiercely. It was a sad sight. Soon she took a list to starboard and slowly went down by the head. The last we saw of her was the Union Jack on the mizzen.

After studying the chart, Captain Jensen told us that we had almost four hundred miles to go. He decided that if the wind held as it was, the best plan was to try for the tip of Nova Scotia around Yarmouth. We put her nose for there.

That night we had our first rationed meal: half a biscuit, one tiny measured portion of water, one slice of corned beef. We had only oars and a small sail which could not make headway for the boat in anything but a fair wind. Realizing that if the wind changed we could be driven farther off-shore and that we might be out a long while, rationing was strict.

Evening brought more wind and a solid drizzle of cold rain which made us miserable. So ended May the 19th.

On the 20th it rained all day. We filled the only containers we could find (two small cans) and drank from cupped hands the water which streamed from the corner of the sail. We all wore oilskins with life jackets over, but the water penetrated everything and left us shivering, miserable, and cramped in the crowded space we had. Several had no southwesters and, to prevent the torrential rain from running down our necks, weird-looking headpieces had been made use of in the form of paper boxes and pieces of canvas. One man had put a huge canvas sea anchor over his head and someone observed that he looked like one of the seven dwarfs. Indeed it was an outlandish crew that huddled in the bottom of the boat. However, the wind was from astern and we were covering eighty miles a day.

The 21st came in with the wind still fair, but stronger. We were making good progress, although the chilling rain still came in occasional squalls, and despite the rubber clothing all hands were completely soaked by this time. The meager rations were anything but tasty, and the corned beef only made us more thirsty, so several of the men gave their portions away.

The 22nd brought no rain, but fast-moving clouds raced across the sky, driven by a wind which had strengthened perceptibly. By noon the wind had dried our clothing and we felt better except that we had to go back to our tiny ration of water. However, we all were cheerful as we watched the pencil line on the captain's chart drawing slowly nearer to Nova Scotia, and several bets came up as to when we would get in. We also expected to sight patrol planes any day now. As it grew dark in the evening of this day, the wind jumped up another notch and we bounded along all night at the maximum speed that the boat was capable of, taking spray aboard which soaked us again.

The 23rd of May brought the last dawn for six of the men. It broke cold and gray with a high sea running and half a gale. We took turns steering, shivered, and gnawed at our biscuits. Nobody cared for this much wind and sea, but all agreed that a few days of it would see us in as far as the patrols. Afternoon saw the wind coming up to gale force, and the seas very long and high. As we skidded from their crests down the long expanse of their sides it reminded me of driving along a hilly countryside road. By four o'clock that afternoon the size of the seas moved Captain Jensen to get the sea anchor ready before dark. At five we let it out with the oil bag attached, but to our disappointment, even with all the lines paid out, the anchor proved too small and for a few minutes the boat lay broadside to the seas. This was very dangerous, so we took down the short spar and with its gaff and boom rigged a triangular sea anchor. This, let out on a 60-fathom line, held the boat's bow nicely into the seas, which were now of tremendous size. After rigging a canvas spray shield forward, we opened the biscuits and water tins and began supper. Before we had started to eat, someone noticed that the bow seemed to be falling away from the wind again. A hand on the sea anchor line found it limp. We were dragging only a piece of rope!

Until now, though we had all realized that the sea was dangerously rough, the prospect of instant disaster had not been present. Now however, with the boat falling off broadside to the huge gray mountains of water which rolled towards us muttering and then broke in an angry roar, we knew that at last the chips were down.

Captain Jensen said grimly, "Row for the sea anchor men; your lives depend on this." We dropped the food, sprang to the oars and tried to make headway into the seas, while Frenchy in the bow strained his eyes ahead into the gathering dusk for the lost spars. Once we rose on the crest of a huge sea and he saw the spars riding on the next wave to windward. We strained every muscle.

One thing I remember plainly while we were straining at the oars. A gull or petrel of some type came so close alongside that I might have struck him with the oar I was wielding. His wings spread motionless, he seemed in the face of the wind to run on the water. I shall remember the bird's webbed feet running up the steep side of the sea. To me the casual and complacent look in his eye seemed an insult.

I believe we fought at the oars for about fifteen minutes, giving all our strength. Once again Frenchy saw the spars, but thought they were farther away. After that he could not see them, and soon darkness set in. We rowed for a while but, as we had no strength to keep the bow into the wind all night, decided on the only thing left. We turned and ran before it. With the captain steering very carefully, we all watched to see how the boat would do. The first grayback lifted us high into the air, and a second later we rushed down its long side like a sled on a hill. Another rose beneath us and again we were off on our wild ride. We relaxed, hoping that the boat would be all right.

Darkness had set in, and most of us had fallen into a sort of shivering doze when we heard the thundering of a monster sea close astern. Shouts of warning, and then the stern of the boat rose up and up into an almost perpendicular wall of water. A second later the wave broke on top of us, the bow dug deep, the stern went up and over, and we were all in the sea amidst a tumult of shouts and rushing water. Seeing the white bottom of the upturned boat, I made for it and struggled aboard with several others. Nearby, Jack, who couldn't swim, was calling for help. A man held the end of an oar and went out after him. Other men were helped up and also the poor dog, which paddled and scratched, panic stricken, at the side. After a moment the captain called out the names and we saw that all were back aboard.

Within five minutes a sea rolled the boat over again, and as the sputtering men climbed back Jack had to be rescued once more. In the darkness it took several minutes to discover that Captain Jensen and his dog were not with us. We called loudly, but heard nothing but the wind and the sea.

Twice more during the next two hours the boat was rolled over and we were thrown into the sea, but all hands managed to climb back. However the filled boat was repeatedly buried under the moving mountains of water, and each time we came up gasping for breath. Jack swallowed a lot of water and became limp and helpless, and about 11 p.m. he died. By this time long immersion in the cold water began to have its effect and all of us were becoming numbed and cramped. As the tragic night wore on, Clar, Cecil, and Sandy passed away. They seemed to sleep, and then toppled over. Shake them as we would, there was no response.

In a desperate search for some means of saving ourselves, we thought of the copper air tanks under the seats. Frank had retained his sheath knife and he, Frenchy, and I tore out a tank and began sawing it in two with the intention of using the ends to bail the boat, and later as containers for rainwater. We took turns at the long and tiresome job, with numb fingers. Presently I saw that Frank had difficulty holding the knife. As dawn was breaking, Frank, my partner and close friend since boyhood, passed away within a few minutes of Frenchy. Later in the morning we who were left said a prayer for our dear shipmates, removed their life jackets, and consigned the bodies into the sea.

With dawn the gale began to drop rapidly. The three men left gazed dully at one another, too shocked to comprehend what had happened. It was evident that the sea was dropping, but for most it came too late. Feeling around the floorboards, we found that all food and gear had been lost except several cans of beef which we jammed back under the floorboards. For eight more hours the mate, the cook, and I sat in a stupor in the washing boat, the cold Atlantic surging over us, waist high.

At three in the afternoon, starting out of a doze, I saw the cook amidships fumbling with some shiny metal objects. As I crawled to investigate the last one went overboard. In delirium the cook had thrown the cans of food over. Within an hour he died.

At about five o'clock we thought the sea had become calm enough to attempt bailing. We made several back-breaking starts, but always a little swell would sweep over the low gunwale. It was discouraging; we suspected that another night in the water would finish us. But apparently whatever fates were responsible had their lust satiated, for soon the sea was calm and we saw our chance. In a mad, furious burst the water level was brought down several inches. We dared not stop, as a swell might come and destroy the result of our efforts, and so struggled on drunkenly. When the boat was half empty we stopped to rest, and the mate and I looked at each other in the beginning of hope. We had a morsel of beef each and returned to work. At 8:30 the boat was dry, riding high and seaworthy. We shook hands and, pulling the rubber clothes and life belts over us, fell into exhausted sleep.

We awoke late in the morning of the 25th to find the sun high and throwing a most welcome warmth. With new hope and strength we tore off a section of the gunwale from each side and set up a crude mast, which we stayed with unraveled strands from a rope. We spread two rubber coats on this and found a pair of trousers which we split and used for a jib. We found, too, the chart with the captain's pencil line marking our daily progress in the boat, ending at the fatal spot marked with X. This line ended a bit short of the southeast edge of George's Bank, well known to fishermen from the United States and Canada. We estimated that even if the wind remained fair, we had several days' sailing at best to reach land.

We found a half-dozen flares, which we laid out in the sun to dry, a first aid kit, and a sewing kit, but no food or water. After the meager ration of water aboard the lifeboat, the salt water swallowed during the gale, and the utter lack of it now, hunger and especially thirst bothered us continually, though not seriously as yet. That night while one slept, the other kept the boat's bow toward the North Star with the steering oar.

May 26th was warm also. The first waking thought was water, but there was no relief. With thread from the sewing kit and safety pins baited with cotton wool as lures, we tried to catch one of the fat curious gulls which circled a foot out of reach of the oar, but they were too wary. Apparently we were on George's, for we saw many fish. Once a loud whirring sound made us turn around to see directly astern a huge school of small silvery fish leaping from the water as if in a cloud, and beneath, the arched backs and dorsal fins of the feeding porpoises. In the bright sunlight of the afternoon we fished again. I dreamed of the hundreds of bubbling brooks which were running on the land over the horizon.

Towards dawn of the 27th the mate, steering, laid his hand upon the seat and felt it come away wet. Tasting the globules of moisture on his palm, he found them fresh. In a moment we were "licking down" seats, gunwales, and every painted surface. It was gratifying, if undignified, and we agreed that hereafter the mate owned the port side, I the starboard.

About dusk that night we suddenly became aware of a faint droning. Straining my eyes, I finally saw the wing lights of a plane passing far to port. Frantically we tried the flares which we had been drying so carefully during the last few days. The first two refused to spark, but the third gave off a brief red light. The green and red lights of the plane continued to move away for a minute and then circled to the left. We uttered a prayer of thanksgiving as the drone grew in intensity, and the plane went over us at such a low altitude that her crew could plainly see us waving our coats. She circled twice, then blinked O.K. with her lights and sped away toward the American coast.

That night we sat up talking, and licked the dew off the boat as soon as it had time to form.

Next morning as we moved slowly before a fresh breeze in the company of half a dozen whales which rolled and blew, sometimes within a few feet of us, a small wisp of smoke on the skyline grew in size and materialized into one of Uncle Sam's new destroyer escorts.

As I looked up into the curious, tanned, healthy young faces lining the rail, I thought in glorious anticipation, "Those guys look as though they have plenty to eat—and some to spare."

The next morning we were put ashore at Portland, Maine.

And that is all there is to tell about the *Angelus* except that I will not forget the boys who did not come back. The fellows on the *Angelus* were not angels. Most of them were rough sailors, but they were open and honest and the best of shipmates.

The America's Cup
War Games

by Frank McNulty

JUNE and JULY, 1963

McNulty was a crew member on Gretel, *the Australian's 1962 challenger.*

Australia started the *War Game of the 1962 America's Cup*—the waging of wits ashore and afloat to pry out information on the "enemy's" equipment and racing form.

But though we started it, the Americans played it, too. The "game" became as integral a part of the 1962 challenge as the races themselves.

The war game began weeks before the main Australian party left Australia for the United States. The Australian syndicate sent a "pilot force" of three men to Newport. Their mission was to study the tactics and techniques of American 12-meters under sail to try to fill in the many wide gaps in our knowledge.

Jock Sturrock and Archie Robertson, then Australia's co-skippers, with veteran Sydney sailmaker Joe Pearce, made up the force. At Newport they hired a fast launch and closely dogged the American yachts day by day. Through binoculars they studied each sail trim and crew maneuver. The day *Columbia* broke her mast they had no need for binoculars, or so the Americans said. The Australian launch was near enough to the yacht to sweep aboard—almost before they got wet—two *Columbia* crewmen who had fallen over the side.

Amid their thanks, the Americans had more to say. "Go ahead. Look us over all you like," they said. "But remember, we'll do just that to you when *Gretel* arrives."

The Americans did, with a vengeance. On each of those warm, often steamy, summer days when *Gretel* put to sea with her trial partner *Vim*, at least one American power boat would follow, watching. At times the launches would close to within fifty feet. They never stood off more than several hundred yards.

The climax came in the week following *Weatherly*'s selection to defend the America's Cup against *Gretel*. Key men of the *Weatherly* crew, in a launch capable of 50 m.p.h., gave *Gretel* the full treatment. For three days, during which *Gretel* spent no less than nine hours at a time on the water, they cruised alongside just out of collision range. Two Americans, including U.S. skipper "Bus" Mosbacher, used binoculars, and two snapped away with 35mm cameras.

Another "gunned" *Gretel* continuously with a polaroid camera that provides almost instant prints. These were torn from the camera back after each exposure and passed to Mosbacher for analysis. The prints showed him the position and duty of each *Gretel* crewman through the craft's complex range of tacking and running maneuvers.

Afloat, the Americans seemed ahead on points in the war game. Ashore, the Australians more than evened the score. To the crew, the biggest Australian secret of the series was the efficiency of *Gretel*'s two main winches, called coffee grinders in sailing circles, and the Americans discovered this efficiency only when it was too late.

The winches were devised and built in Sydney as part of a syndicate experiment with £10,000 to try to improve on the American winches and other deck equipment that had arrived in Australia on *Vim* and were in use aboard her. The Australian winches, of alloy and steel with drums or capstans 14 inches across, do the heavy "pully-hauley" work aboard. They control the wire rope to the big headsail under a strain of several tons, and the huge billowing nylon spinnakers which can tug into the air two, even three men.

A secret of the new Australian coffee grinders was that we could set four men together to wind the handles that operate them. Only two men—half the power—could operate the American-designed winches. In addition, the Australian winches had gears to give three speeds, whereas the American had only two gears.

The success of the Australian machines in Sydney Harbor trials so impressed the syndicate that it had engineers block out one of three gears to reduce their power. The syndicate then put around the story, even to crewmen who were to accompany *Gretel* to the United States, that the winches were "trouble boxes." An inference was that they might be put ashore at any time. This story undoubtedly got back to America. It may have allayed any American fears that we possessed a "secret weapon," but it diminished by little their curiosity about these angular, almost unsightly devices with their novel foot-change gear pedals.

In Newport, after we settled in at the Castle Hill Hotel, a regular fraternization with our American counterparts began. This continued through the eight weeks of training and the actual America's Cup races. In that time I rarely met an American crewman who didn't lead the conversation to *Gretel*'s winches. Others of our crew found it the same. This became the era of double-talk. The Australian would dismiss his winches with, "Well, we are never fully happy with them . . . All that junk inside must increase the chance of a breakdown." True, if you want to analyze the statement, but pure double-talk.

Once a senior man of the *Weatherly* camp showed open anger. He accused us of using underhanded methods to gain information, and called a fellow American a traitor. The "traitor," not a member of *Weatherly*'s crew, had revealed to two Australian friends certain techniques in trimming mainsails and spinnakers which the Americans had evolved and adopted since the last America's Cup races, in 1958. This information was passed on in fewer than fifty words and helped revolutionize *Gretel*'s speed when sailing with the wind behind her. It was information that our close observers of the early American trials had almost no hope of stumbling upon, even with their binoculars.

Then our camp got a good technological boost. The ocean waters on which the races are held are known for their wind shifts, sudden changes in wind strength, and, perhaps the greatest hazard of all to the novice sailing them, flash fogs.

On a bright clear day these fogs roll low across the sea like dense smoke from a coal-burning tug. They blot out boats, sky, and shoreline. They reduce visibility to less than a hundred yards and have cost many a race when a yacht has failed to find the correct rounding mark. In one American race the leader, suddenly enveloped, missed the finish line.

As an insurance against getting lost and to put us one jump ahead of the Americans, the Australian syndicate arranged for *Gretel* to use a British electronic navigation device.

This, a Decca system, was far more accurate than a comparable American unit, and it was virtually unknown there. Several *Gretel* men had been told in whispers of this device; others had overheard talk that added up to its existence. On an appointed day, two of our camp—Terry Hammond of Brisbane and Magnus Halvorsen of Sydney—put on their blazers as the rest of us stepped into our sailing gear for another day on the water. These two then headed for New York, some two hundred miles from Newport, to spend two days learning to operate the device at the office of its agent.

"Would you believe it," our teammates told us later. "There, waiting in the office to do the course with us, were two *Weatherly* crewmen." Somehow, the Americans had overheard, too. They had moved fast and arranged to fit the same Decca unit. We laughed. It was all in the game.

In a way I'm glad the Americans did find out. *Weatherly* used her Decca navigation device in the five races against *Gretel* and this, in theory, put us on an equal footing in navigation. And to a degree it removed from the challenge a phase of endeavor that is least in the spirit of sport: the advantage one side can gain by spending big money or by using a technological advance unknown to the other.

Castle Hill Hotel, known variously to us as "the pub with no beer" and "Alcatraz," was our home for the three months of Australia's attempt to take home the America's Cup. In two- to four-bed rooms, off corridors rambling over three floors, we unpacked on that first day in Newport, then set out to meet and discover America.

On the first five minutes' walk along old Newport's cobbled streets, during that first pale, weak beer in a sidewalk bar, we realized we were "in." There were friendship and smiles and welcome on every side. For this, no doubt, we had to thank the reputation and personalities of the many Australian sportsmen who had visited America before us—these and the hundreds of thousands of Americans who came home after World War II with more than a soft spot for Australia and Australian hospitality.

That was just the beginning for us. In a short time the hospitality extended by Americans, and the offers of more received at Castle Hill, led one of our syndicate nabobs to say, "This is barely short of sabotage of the crew." Hospitality to a visitor is one thing. Few of us were prepared for our next discovery.

Many people we met in this country of quite intense national pride—in a land, so we believed, of the bad loser—actually wanted to see Australia win the America's Cup.

"We've had the goddamn Cup too long," said one.

"We're too sure of ourselves. We should lose it for a time to revive the interest," was another.

A worker at the waterfront supported us to the hilt, perhaps for another reason.

"Don't think you're here to race America," he said. "You're up against those rich guys of the New York Yacht Club. Every worker in the country is on your side."

Our meeting with the "natives" and, ultimately, our virtual assimilation, was not without some setbacks. American idiom has many traps for the Australian. Several everyday Australian expressions, even single words, have meanings in America that are definitely not for the drawing room. Others convey an entirely different meaning from that intended.

A prime example of this was the arrest of an Australian photographer, attached to a film unit to cover the races, when he asked innocently if he could get "an angle shot at the President." American police construed his word "shot" to mean he wanted to assassinate Mr. Kennedy. The photographer's arrest was our introduction to security-consciousness in America.

We take security measures with VIP's in Australia, and probably to the same degree, but nowhere have I seen security so evident as in America. The day we were received by President and Mrs. Kennedy at Newport is a good example.

A list of names of *Gretel* men was approved by Newport's police chief, and then the contingent—twenty-four of the *Vim* and *Gretel* crews and reserves, five specialists and syndicate members—left Castle Hill in cars bound for Hammersmith Farm. This is the home of Mrs.

Kennedy's family, where she and President Kennedy often spent part of their summer holidays. The three-story stone and brick home, large as it is, is "a weekender" in Newport parlance. It is one of sixty or seventy comparable glorious homes with sweeping waterfrontages and views, all three to four miles from the hurly-burly port town of Newport itself.

Hammersmith Farm is set on some fifty acres of closely cropped lawn and carefully trimmed bushes, and the drive from the front gate to the home is 350 yards. At the gate a policeman in uniform and two plainclothesmen stopped us. They insisted that the syndicate head, Sir Frank Packer, personally vouch for each Australian. And Sir Frank stood by the roadside, peering into each car and nodding as the plainclothes gents called to him the name of each one of us.

A hundred yards up the drive, on an almost hairpin bend, a gent stood up from behind a hedge, his right hand inside his suit coat in an almost Napoleonic stance. We speculated on what his hand might hold, then began to discuss idly what penalty rates an FBI guard might get in rain or snow for an eight-hour shift in a hedge.

The cars pulled up before the Hammersmith Farm homestead. The head of a man appeared above a bush only twenty feet away. Then with the aplomb of a junior executive, he drew to him a telephone handset from a nearby tree.

For the first few minutes inside Hammersmith Farm—throughout the first two drinks, to be exact—I had the distinct feeling that to put a hand hurriedly into my pocket or to begin to run might be the last thing I'd ever do.

Twenty minutes later the Kennedys entered and banished that feeling completely. None of us knew what form our introduction would take, and several had visions of being lined up like a soccer team on a field to have hands shaken individually by the dignitaries.

It happened quite differently. The President and Mrs. Kennedy chatted briefly with Mrs. Kennedy's mother and her husband, Mr. Hugh Auchincloss. Then they split up and "did" the room.

In an atmosphere less stiff than the average cocktail party, they spoke individually to almost every Australian. They asked questions, the questions you would expect of any person to whom you had just been introduced—"Where are you from?" and "How do you like sailing in these waters?" and "What do you do in the crew?"

It could not have been more friendly. Great honor as it was to be received by the President and First Lady of the United States, we came to feel no awe as many, perhaps properly, would have. We came to feel that Mr. and Mrs. Kennedy, both lovers of sailing, were glad to meet us, and we were more than happy to meet them. This day marked the height of our social attainment in the United States. Indeed, it would have been difficult to go higher.

But Australia's greatest day—to an Australian—was the victory in the second race against *Weatherly*. It was the day Skipper Jock Sturrock had the 29 tons of *Gretel* surfing down the face of several seas, and the day the efficiency of our winches was revealed for the first time to the *Weatherly* crew.

I was a winch-hand. It was a glorious day. In a tacking duel in which both yachts switched course eleven times in five minutes, *Gretel* savaged *Weatherly*. Our winches trimmed in *Gretel*'s headsail to its proper setting seconds in advance of *Weatherly* each time. The result was that *Gretel* caught up to *Weatherly*, eliminating the lead the American boat had previously been widening. And *Weatherly* never again engaged *Gretel* in a tacking duel.

Newspapers reported this duel as a triumph for the muscled Australian winchmen. We were tigers . . . strong as bears. But I've already told you the secret. Four men could man the *Gretel* winches—only two the American winches on *Weatherly*.

I learned later that in the frenzy of those minutes the Americans managed to squeeze onto their winch handles a total of "two-and-a-half" men. Let me add, though, that I believe *Gretel*'s winchmen were stronger and fitter than their American counterparts.

Race Three was on a light, fluky day and *Weatherly* went on to win by 8 minutes 40 seconds, at one time having held a lead of more than 23 minutes over *Gretel*. This was the day Jock Sturrock made his major tactical error. *Weatherly* rounded the first mark in a dying wind only 58 seconds ahead. *Gretel* was still, as they say, in a handy position.

Standard race tactics dictated that *Gretel* should have stayed right on the tail of the leader in the hope that her sails might cut off the leader's wind. *Gretel* should at least have stayed with the boat ahead and done all in her power not to lose more time. Only when a yacht has no hope of catching the leader should she take the gamble of setting a different course which might, coincidentally, expose her to different winds. Sturrock breached the rule and gambled on a course of his own.

Gretel sailed into a gaping hole in the wind and stopped with every sail sagging. *Weatherly* continued to meander on towards the next mark in the lightest of breezes, to our added frustration.

In the fourth race, the closest sailed in the history of the America's

Cup, *Gretel* fell for the perfect dummy, and lost the chance to win. Both boats were sailing under spinnakers in the last half-mile of the 24-mile race. *Weatherly* was about 150 yards ahead, and *Gretel* was closing fast. At this moment Bus Mosbacher did the unpredictable.

In doing it he exposed the great depth of resource he commands—the reason why he is the greatest living helmsman in the United States and perhaps the world.

Mosbacher took off his spinnaker, cutting his boat's speed by one-third. *Gretel*, assuming that *Weatherly* had spied a shift of wind which would make the spinnaker a handicap, followed suit.

Gretel's spinnaker came down and *Gretel*'s pace slackened. But no change of wind occurred sufficient to justify the dropping of the sail.

There is an analogy in speedcars. Two are on the final straight to the finish with the second car overtaking at a rate that could win it the race. The leader suddenly slams on his brakes. What should the second car do? Should its driver continue hell-bent for the finish, or should he also brake in case something is amiss on the road ahead? *Gretel* braked. Nothing ahead was amiss. *Gretel* had been duped.

I've skippered racing boats on Sydney Harbor for twenty-three years, and I've read and talked a lot about sailing. Never have I heard of a maneuver—and it was a gamble, too—like that. Mr. Mosbacher, we've got to hand it to you.

So we lost the race, and the series, 4-1. But the 1962 challenge did provide one great moment for the Australian crew—the moment every man will recall in crisp detail even in his late wheelchair days. It was when *Gretel* plunged down the face of the first of several seas to pass *Weatherly* in that second race.

Gretel's speed almost doubled the instant she began to shoot the wave. One crewman let out a "Yeehooo" of exhilaration. At least eight others joined in at full blast.

On our deck no more than sixty feet away from *Weatherly*, one *Gretel* man grabbed a rope end and began flaying the side of the flying yacht in the perfect simulation of a jockey riding a tight Ranwick finish.

What would Sir Thomas Lipton have said!

The Fiberglass
Invasion

by Joe Richards

AUGUST, 1966

Princess, *a 25-foot Friendship sloop, was once described by her owner as "mistress, mother, constant companion, artist's model, friend of the family, millstone, and rat hole into which has gone uncounted quantities of loot." Richards, a frequent contributor to the magazine in the 1960s and '70s, was described by a* Rudder *editor as "character, painter, artist, author, boatman, whirlwind."*

Princess lay all night in an open roadstead off Bimini. She swooped into every phosphorescent sea at the end of her cable as she ran the endless unrecorded miles of a vessel at anchor. I watched the strewn sea in the black night, and I wondered how many times around the world all those miles would tally in the life of a boat.

I thought of all the boats and all the hours and all the miles that were spent at a mooring or a dock going nowhere. And all the poor slobs that were spoiling to go and all the romantic places that they would never get to.

As *Princess* surged against the sea I hit the sack, tired as hell and maybe a little smug. I had come at least this far. We were anchored off a foreign port. I sailed into sleep as the first green fire of a tropical day cut the crystal water.

In the last hour of darkness the wind went into the east. We were in the lee of land. The anchor was holding on a hundred feet of chain. *Princess* swung gently between the soft persuasion of the wind and the nudge of the current. I slept late.

Lennie slept on deck under the dinghy. The kids woke him, chattering on the cabin top. When I came on deck the sun had come over the hill and the day unfolded like some kind of blue-green flower. Shiny and clear.

Lennie and Seth were over the side. Big bearded Lennie and my kid were somewhere down below in a sea so transparent that it was a wonder they didn't figure it for air and toss their masks away.

The water was so clear that you could see the floor of coral at forty feet as if it was the Bimini blue bottom of our bathtub back on 50th Street.

There was the anchor caught in kelp. There was a school of jack followed by a pokey grouper. There was a little fellow with a yellow diving mask trailing a big guy with a black mask and a coal black beard.

We had breakfast ready for them when they lifted their Hawaiian slings, laid them on the deck, and jumped on board.

Suzy was watching the coral ridge through the glass. She ran her eyes along the sugary sand, over the little houses on the hill, and down to the point. She sensed the whiteness of everything against the bluest of blues and the jet black people that made it all sing. We could hardly wait to get ashore.

Bacon and eggs off Bimini is like bacon and eggs anywhere else where the air is totally free of dust, the sky full of nothing but blue, and the water simply a deeper shade of sky that seems to support the boats in a tricky gambol.

Princess was a long way from Pugsley Creek, Bronx, New York. This was no Eastchester Bay. To goof this up with the thought of polluted rivers and contaminated bays would have been to spoil our breakfast in particular and to louse up the feast in general.

We sat there munching in stupefaction, wondering why a native of this place would ever emigrate. Or how long it would be before the rest of the world was climbing on their backs.

There was no one on their backs on that fine third day of July in 1963. Not even the scenery stiffs that arrive early in the afternoon and leave before dark. The vessel that makes regular runs between Miami and Bimini was in drydock over on the mainland. She had run aground and she sprung some planks trying to negotiate the millrace of the new channel. No wonder. You could see the reason from a hundred yards away.

We elected to run around the point, and we found the feeble little range of lights that can bring you into the harbor of Bimini at night. If you know where it is. Or how to find it.

There isn't enough in Bimini at night to make it worth the danger. It is better to come in during the hours of daylight. There is a lot to see. The sunlight on the shoal danced in the constant exuberance of the surf, and it bounced in all the shades of shell. We ran the violent current into the limited harbor, bearing close along the docks of the eating dives. We caught hold of a piling at the Angler's Club and gas dock.

A very formal immigration officer in a uniform that smacked of a British Bobby checked us in. This cat made all sorts of vital notations on a form that was struggling to take off from his clipboard in the determined easterly while we rocked on the dock in the persistant reverberations of a day, a night, and half another day in a little boat.

At last he ran out of red tape and he gave us a great white smile as if the whole business was a big joke dreamed up by some clown in the Foreign Office for the amusement of the natives.

We walked the streets of the little colonial town. Bimini looked like Miami might have looked in the 1880s. Or Coconut Grove. There were little wooden inns and tiny shops filled with tourist trash and all the junk made in Podunk that traveling people buy to send back where it came from. There were shops that sold food at twice the mainland price and shops that sold liquor at less than half of it.

We walked along the cusp of a ridge that was at least as high as the outcroppings along Bayshore Drive in Miami. From that height you could see the long shoals to the southeast that spawn the fish and all the tiny uninhabited islands that lay between Bimini and Gun Cay.

That was the way to go. When we got down to *Princess*, the kids had found the aquarium. The sharks were nicely fenced off. So were the porpoises. There was none of that dog-eat-dog freedom that you find in the garment district. We waited in the shade of the palms for the bread to bake in the smallest bakery in the world. It was worth waiting for. We found a freshwater shower on the gas dock hidden in the head. We left Bimini showered and/or shaved. *Princess* was loaded with Dutch beer, newly baked bread, fresh water, ice, and new straw hats for all hands. The wind was on the port beam and strong. We sailed due south.

We sailed half the afternoon against a current that must have been the first cousin of the Gulf Stream. The wind at least was in our favor. We skirted Turtle Rocks, bearing to the west lest the current carry us in among the shoals. We ran close aboard Piquet Rock, scaring some gulls into tiny scudding flecks of white that got lost in the covey of little clouds.

It was a long two-hour run by the time we came abreast of Holm Cay and headed for the lighthouse on the south end of Gun Cay. The sun was deep in the west. An oblique ray of light like the burst of sun in a painting by some groovey old master struck a patch of beach that was so white, so clean, and came on so strong that we stared in silence. *Princess*, sailing herself, edged over to the east, heading tentatively in between the north end of Gun Cay and a friendly little rock that rose just north of it.

So kindly was the aspect of the place that we let her go. The kids were out on the bowsprit and so was Lennie with a lead line when we entered the tiny cove. The entrance from the west was unobstructed. The bottom was apparent. There were no pinnacles of coral, and it shoaled easy toward the beach.

As we wheeled in the cove and came about, *Princess* made an unmistakable curtsy and dropped her hook. Her sails shivered in excitement as we let them go. This was her pad. She was home.

This was the island we were looking for. The Caribbean island that had everything. It fitted the dream as if it was poured into it.

There was the cove of sand cupping the clear water with a boomerang-shaped beach soft as down. There was the lithe little grove of palms, and to the north against the weather was the reef of rock jeweled by the sea. There was even an abandoned little house on the hill. The roof shed rainwater into a huge iron drum. The place was jumping with fish.

As the kids went over the side, I thought of all the islands and all the coves and all the wartime places here and in the Pacific that I had found and left. I held Betty's hand in all this soulful jazz and wondered if she minded having *Princess* along.

As far as *Princess* was concerned, it was hardly as cosy as it might have been without my wife, the kids, and Lennie along. But it was all she could ask for in the way of an island. Except for getting us back safely, she had completed her function.

This was it. It was what John Charlton calls "awful pretty country." But damn near all the prettiness is under water. Betty and I put on our masks and joined Lennie and the kids to see it.

Don't take my word for it. No configuration of canyon and cliff, no volcanic panorama, no cascade of water spilling into a deep and misty valley, no outdoor wonder can beat the kind of merchandise we were looking at. Betty and I finished the day chasing shadow and substance, the shimmer and the shade and all the cockeyed wonder of underwater life. It was better than Bonwit's window on the night before Christmas. The kids were more businesslike.

They speared a mess of snappers, blues, and crawfish. Lennie came up with a baby octopus. We showered with the water from the cistern on the hill, and Lennie opened his great big sea bag.

Out of it came a cauldron, his pet sauce pan, and spices for which the conquistadores would have sailed halfway around the world. We had bouillabaisse on the beach and a seafood smorgasbord to put to shame the cuisine of Agostino himself.

Down the beach a little motorboat pulled in from Lauderdale. They were real polite. They declined to join us. They squatted to the lee and tasted ham sandwiches with their tongues while their noses devoured the aroma. Lennie, full of Dutch beer and his own masterwork, curled around the driftwood fire as the sun went down and fell asleep. There was a full moon. Naturally.

The next day was the quietest Fourth of July we had ever known. It was one of the quietest days we have ever known. There was no way to celebrate the victory over the British except by occupying this tiny patch of heaven that we had forgotten to take away from them. The motorboat left in the morning and we were alone. We had a sneaking suspicion that there were other people who knew about this place, but we paid it no mind.

We lolled in the sun and chased the phantom fish for fun and food. We searched the grottos of the reef for lobsters, and we dove for conch. We ate the pure white meat of it with a touch of lime juice. Lennie found some turtle eggs. The kids from Lauderdale had destroyed most of them out of devilment, but we had a seafood omelet for breakfast. The day slipped away full of everything but war and business and scientific achievement and crime. It was too good to last.

Suddenly out of nowhere there were a half-dozen Boston Whalers on the beach, full of boxes and baskets and umbrellas and drums and guitars and God knows what all.

The umbrellas popped open, the tables were unfolded, and the bongo drummer began to swing it. And from everywhere came boats. Great big fancy marlin fishing boats, like a hundred of them, clustering around *Princess* in the tiny harbor like a free day at the boat show.

Then it started—the Calypso music and the talk and the mountain of food and the drinks. For two bucks each we were happy to join the gang. The kids ate free. In fact, they were lost among the people and the people and the people.

This was the day of the annual outing of the chowder-chomping, whiskey-belting, hell-for-leather Marlin Fishing Club. Our little island was the scene.

We made it.

Masters of
the Jury Rig

by Steve Gantry

MARCH, 1969

The boat was a mass of flame, and thick, greasy smoke poured from her engine compartment. Don Aronow hastily launched an inflated life raft on the lee side of the bow and stepped aboard. His mechanic, "Knocky" House, joined him. House was bleeding badly from a cut.

It was the end of their bid to win the 1968 Miami-Nassau race—which they were leading at the time. A fuel tank split three miles out of Nassau, and their remaining gas burst into flames. They had launched the raft on the boat's lee side, and the raft's sea anchor held them tight against the burning boat.

"We were suffocating from the smoke, and it was getting pretty hot," Knocky recalled. "I pulled out my pocketknife—I always carry one—and cut the anchor line. Then we paddled the hell out of there."

House was still bleeding. Aronow looked at him for a moment. "Stop bleeding," he said. "I think there are sharks following us."

The anecdote underscores a hitherto unheralded fact of ocean powerboat racing: It is often the mechanic who meets the emergency with his fist clenched around a tool—even a humble pocketknife. The winning driver gets his name in the papers, but even the most avid fans rarely know that it was an unsung mechanic who put him there.

Don Pruett is a good example. A 6-foot-4 Texan, Pruett has ridden as mechanic and co-driver with Vincenzo Balestrieri, while the Italian sportsman wrapped up last year's international offshore championship.

Pruett's labors helped in the Naples race early in the season. "We broke an exhaust valve," Pruett recalled. "Oil pressure dropped. The engine would go pretty quick." Pruett crawled back into the engine compartment, braced himself as comfortably as he could, and began opening oil cans.

"I guess I sat there and poured oil for a hundred miles," he said. Anyone who has opened an engine hatch and felt the blast of heat and noise inside can appreciate what Pruett endured while Balestrieri grimly pushed for a victory and another step toward the world title.

Early in the 1967 race at Cowes, England, a fuel tank had ruptured and filled the bilges with raw gas. Pruett was riding with Thunderbird executive Bob Rodman at the time.

"It was kinda foolish," Pruett recalled, "but in the excitement of a race, you do almost anything to keep the boat going."

Even though the gas-filled boat was a floating bomb, Pruett switched on the bilge pumps. The gas made the impellers swell up, and they jammed. He still had to get the gas out of the bilges. So Pruett crawled into the engine compartment and disconnected the cooling water intake hose.

"I stuck my foot over the hull intake to block the water," he said, "and then I stuck the engine intake hose down into the gas in the bilges."

Pruett calmly sat on top of a potential bomb while the engine's water pump sucked raw gas out of the bilges, circulated it through the engine like cooling water, and spat it out the exhaust. Oddly enough, it wasn't an explosion that lost the race. They ran out of gas.

Fate caught up to Pruett in the 1968 Nassau race—the same one in which Aronow and Knocky House abandoned their burning boat. Again, it was gas in the bilges, plus stalled engines.

"I had a bad cold," said Pruett. "Couldn't smell a thing. I crawled back in the engine compartment, didn't smell the gas, tried the electric fuel pumps and saw that we had fuel pressure, so I hit the starter solenoid button."

It blew. The explosion sent Pruett flying back into the cockpit, but he was able to grab the CO_2 extinguisher system handle and douse the flames.

Pruett was badly burned on his face, chest, and arms. Balestrieri didn't speak English and couldn't use the radio to call for help. Fortunately, outboard racer Jim Harkins saw their boat lying dead in the water, stopped, and got help. Minutes later a Coast Guard helicopter had Pruett aboard and enroute to a hospital in Miami. Three weeks later he got out of the hospital, borrowed a boat from Balestrieri, and won the Miami-Key West race, his first stab at driving.

But crawling into the engine compartment during a race, though it sounds like Pruett's hobby, is nothing novel for mechanics. Another practitioner is Sammy James, special projects engineer for Bertram-Nautec. The impressive-sounding title means James is the racing mechanic for company president Peter Rittmaster in races like the Bahamas 500—the toughest ocean race on the books. Salt water got to Rittmaster's engines as he and James neared the finish line in the 1967 running.

"It was rough," recalled James, "and pitch black. We kept coming off the top of waves, and we couldn't even see. Finally one engine died."

With a navigator holding a flashlight, James crawled into the engine compartment and dried off the distributor. Rittmaster got the engine started, and the boat took off. The navigator dropped his flashlight when Rittmaster punched the throttles open, and Sammy was stuck in the dark engine compartment next to a pair of roaring engines.

"I wasn't about to crawl out over the shafts," he said, "so I made myself as comfortable as I could."

Soon the salt water got to the engine again; it died, and the boat wallowed down off plane.

"I waited a few minutes and then cleaned the distributor again," James said. "And Rittmaster took off."

He finished the race, alternately bracing himself and wiping the dstributor, perched awkwardly in the engine compartment.

Few tales, though, match Sammy's experience with an overheating V-drive. It was in the 1968 Bahamas 500. Rittmaster had gotten as far as Nassau when Sammy found the V-drive temperature was up to about 300 degrees. It was only a matter of time before the drive blew.

"You can't dip up a bucket of sea water at sixty miles an hour," observed Sammy. So James sat down and pulled open the big ice chest. He started pouring ice water slowly over the V-drive. When the water was gone, he began opening soft drinks and pouring them slowly over the V-drive, nursing each one as long as he could.

"Peter asked me for one of the drinks while they were still cold," said James. " 'The hell with you,' I said. 'These are for the V-drive.' "

Between the melted ice and soft drinks aboard, James was able to keep the drive gears cool enough for Rittmaster to finish third. It was worth being thirsty.

It was in a race in the Pacific that Knocky House and Don Aronow established a new first for ocean racing—they hit a helicopter. Florida racers find the Pacific with its high, stretched-out seas a little wild. Aronow jumped off one giant swell so high into the air that the boat rammed a low-flying chopper carrying news photographers. Amazingly, the only damage was some chrome scraped off a cleat on the boat's bow.

It was in another Pacific race (to Catalina Island) that House joined the engine compartment set. Oil was pouring out the breathers and salt water was getting into the crankcase.

"I had to practically wrap myself around the engine to start pouring oil into it," he said afterward, "but it was the only engine we had."

Aronow had to pass the oil back from the cockpit while running the boat, and House said he went through twelve quarts of oil—all of which went straight through the engine—in the last seventy-five miles of the race. But they finished second.

"We were the greasiest, sorriest sights you ever saw," said House.

One of the more cautious mechanics—if anyone in the ocean-racing powerboat game can be called "cautious"—is Bobby Moore, who crews for boatbuilder Jake Trotter. In the 1966 Miami-Nassau, Trotter's fuel tank split, luckily on a seam fairly well above the tank bottom. Moore crawled aft and stuffed a towel into the opening in the tank. It stopped most of the fuel splash—except when Trotter jumped the boat off a sea and it landed with a sharp shock. To get the raw gas that had already escaped out of the bilges, Moore disconnected the outlet hose from the V-drive cooling system and stuck it down into the bilges, so sea water mixed with the raw gas. Then he opened the transom drain so the water-gas mix flowed out through the transom. While the bilge was draining, Moore stretched out and hung on at the gunwale.

"If she blew up," recalled Trotter, "Bobby wanted to go overboard easily." He didn't have to, though, and the boat finished third overall.

In the same race a year earlier, Trotter's mechanic was Tommy Mottola. Mottola's workday began when the engine blew a piston. Gas got into the crankcase, and some of it wound up in the bilges. It blew.

"Blew me right overboard," Trotter remembered. "Fortunately, the boat was going very slowly, and I hung on for a few seconds and shouted to Tommy to throw me a rope."

Mottola looked at Trotter in the water and then at the fire the blast had started.

"He put the fire out first," said Trotter.

To solve the piston problem, Mottola dug out a battery-powered drill, drilled down through the spark plug, used the plug as a nipple for a piece of hose, and stuck it in the mechanic's favorite place for hoses—the bilge. The gas and water from the bad cylinder were rammed down into the bilges and out the drain.

Trotter is not a mechanic, but he has been blown into the sea more than once. In the 1967 race to Nassau he and mechanic Dave Stirrat suddenly found themselves in the shark-infested Gulf Stream, swimming about in life jackets while their boat—life raft still aboard—burned not far away.

"In the middle of all this," Trotter recalled, "we didn't get out a Mayday or anything—weren't really sure we'd be seen, even—Dave swims over to me and starts talking about the next race boat we're going to build."

Mechanics are like that. They think only of keeping the engines and boat going; and if the boat fails, they think of the changes they'll make in the next try. But always they meet an emergency with imagination, guts, and probably a wrench in one hand. Take Eddie Booth, a mechanic who rode with John Raulerson some years ago.

Engine trouble and a loss of r.p.m. made it impossible for them to get up and stay on plane. Booth grabbed a crescent wrench, jumped overboard, and pulled pitch out of the propellers until the sick engines could jump the boat up on top. They finished the race. And it was Booth, in another race, who calmly poured lubricating oil into his diesels when they ran out of fuel, keeping the engines going until they crossed the finish line.

But no one really hears of the masters of the jury rig—unless, maybe, they step out of character and win a race. Mel Riggs, a quiet, 30-year-old mechanic from Fond du Lac, Wisconsin, was the first to break the ice. He won the 1968 Miami-Nassau race, and, like Pruett, he did it the first time he ever took the helm in offshore competition.

Riggs doesn't recall any special adventures in the years he raced offshore as mechanic for Odell Lewis. He does remember one Pacific Ocean event off California when he rode with Johnny Bakos.

"We had to go overboard and change the propellers," Riggs remembered. "Then, after we got back in the boat and took off, we ran right through a school of sharks a hundred yards away."

"That," he said, "is the only thing I really remember from the races."

No racer has ever run into shark trouble, and we certainly hope none of them ever does. But if it does happen someday, you can bet one thing: If there's a mechanic involved, he'll just clout the shark on the snout with an open-ended wrench—and finish the race.

Sailfish Showdown
off Stuart

by Jim Wright

APRIL, 1976

To look at the armada lined up at the Bay Harbor Club docks in Stuart, Florida, you'd think German U-boats had just been sighted in the Gulf Stream. Baby destroyers all, with rocket launchers on standby alert, they're being primed for the big four-day battle that begins tomorrow.

The occasion for this naval display is the 22nd annual Stuart Light-Tackle Sailfish Tournament. The time is early December, when sailfish flock to the Gulf Stream off nearby St. Lucie Inlet like Christmas shoppers to Fifth Avenue. To celebrate their arrival, Stuart hosts the foremost sailfish tourney in the world.

Most of the top rod-slingers in the continental United States are on hand to chase a billfish or two—fishing notables the likes of Eleanor Bartlett Reid, the Queen Victoria of tourney royalty; Joe Lopez, 1975's best international release angler; Arthur S. Lazarus, Bahamian angler of the year; and Gloria Applegate, one of the globe's fisherwomen *non pareil*.

These hook-setting virtuosos—more than a hundred in all—have spared no expense to reel in their quarry. Ryboviches, Hatterae, Bertrams, Whiticars, a Merritt or two—checkbook angling at its best. And these 45-footers and 53-footers are mere vestpocket sportfishermen compared to *BoAnn*, a custom 65-foot aluminum fishing catamaran with a cockpit the size of a squash court and, believe it or not, gold faucets in the shape of swans in the master stateroom.

But so it goes with big-time tournament fishing. Blame it on the Easter Parade mentality. Every boat here is dressed to the hilt, and pity the poor chump who doesn't have Fin-Nor or Penn reels and custom-built outriggers.

As for the anglers themselves, they really don't have any common denominator other than that they aren't hurting for bucks and they like to catch sailfish. Thin, tall, fat, small, so-called international sportsmen, rich kids, and plain old fishing fanatics, they've all spent up to $125 apiece in hopes of winning a hunk of walnut with a barometer imbedded in it or having their name engraved on the Captain William Todt Memorial Trophy, which won't buy you a cup of coffee outside the Bay Harbor Club.

Bernard Muckenfuss, captain of *Maverick*, is one of the dedicated hired guns on hand at the docks the afternoon before the fireworks begin. Right now he's testing the line tension on his Penn Internationals (all tourney anglers are required to use 20-pound-test line, and the monofilament will snap if there's too much tension in the reel) and working his way through a can or two of beer. Dressed in khaki and built like a welterweight a couple of years past prime, Bernard is getting the 31-foot Bertram and its gear shipshape for the big shoot-out ahead.

Mention sportfishing boats to Muckenfuss and he eyes *Maverick* with a look that Roy Rogers reserves only for Trigger. "All she was made for is to catch fish," he says proudly.

When you consider that this is a release tourney, that the sailfish are tagged and turned loose (making the event popular with both conservationists and billfish), the money expended in hopes of having a half-dozen sails nuzzle the transom for a few seconds is staggering. The irony doesn't faze Muckenfuss, who discusses the economics of tournament fishing like a man from H & R Block explaining the short form. His boat costs $65,000. The trip from his home port of Charleston, South Carolina, to Stuart and back means $850 in fuel bills alone. Every rod and reel on *Maverick*, and there is a gaggle of them, runs about $450.

"You can't go fishing with Mickey Mouse stuff," explains the intense Mr. M., "because if you've got sixty-five grand in a boat and burn all that fuel and expend all that energy, you don't want to lose a fish because of poor equipment."

Nobody has statistics on how many fish are lost annually on account of bum reels, but at a prestigious gathering such as this, nobody in his or her right mind is going to show up at the dock with Popeil's Pocket Fisherman and a can of dead nightcrawlers.

Which, in *Maverick*'s case, brings up the $65,000 question. Why all the commotion over a chinless, relatively small billfish that Mrs. Paul wouldn't even use for fishsticks?

Granted, there is a stupid variety of sailfish that wouldn't get many anglers out of bed in the morning. *Istiophorus Americanus ignoramus* has a reputation for snapping up bait and then swimming madly *toward* the boat like a lemming in search of a cliff. Dumb. But in a tournament where the angler with the most fish wins, this type of fish is tolerated—if not often preferred.

Then there is his smarter brother. This fish is a feisty fighter. Pure guerrilla. He likes to stun his prey with a lightning stroke of his bill, drop back momentarily, and then, just maybe, move in for the kill. If the prey happens to have a hook and 150 yards of 20-pound-test attached to it, a sailfish can yank the line out of a free-spooling reel at up to 50 m.p.h. If he hasn't spit out the bait or snapped the monofilament when the angler puts on the brake, it's time for acrobatics worthy of Olga Korbut—somersaults, leaps, and spirals. Quite a nifty fish on light tackle.

Sailfish roam Florida waters the whole year round, but they have a predilection for the Gulf Stream between Boynton Beach and Stuart in December and January. Along this stretch, the stream arches only a mile offshore before making an abrupt turn northward at Stuart. A fortuitous blend of wind, temperature, and ocean geography brings together *en masse* sails and the baitfish they feed on, and Stuart becomes the sailfishing capital of the world for a few weeks.

By tournament week in early December, the area is already swarming with sailfish. Trying to catch one of these silver and deep-purple beauties is another matter. The first obstacle is that sailfish are basically bottom fish. Before you can hook 'em, you've got to draw them up from the depths (they usually feed in water 80 to 120 feet deep) with a combination of the right baits, lures, and trolling speeds. Live bait is verboten during the tourney, so fishermen offer a menu of recently deceased balao, mullet, or artificial bait. The other problem is that smart sailfish are more finicky than a three-year-old with a plate of asparagus. They like to play with their food. So when a sailfish hits a line and pulls it off an outrigger or a clothespin set-up on the transom, standard angling procedure is to count to ten and then set the hook with a measured jerk of the rod.

Once the hook is firmly implanted in the fish's jaw, it's a question of brains rather than brawn, the ability to nurse the quarry boatward without snapping the line. It is exactly for this reason that so many of the world's top sailfish anglers are women: They have mastered the art of out-finessing the sailfish, while many of the men insist on trying to out-muscle it.

If William Tecumseh Sherman had to keep marching once he reached the sea, he'd have undoubtedly said that "war is fishing" or something to that effect. Successful tournament sailfishing requires the same sort of meticulous planning that marks a victorious military maneuver—well-drilled troops, accurate scouting reports, and finely tuned equipment. Given the tremendous initial investment, you can't simply throw a pound of frozen bait in the cooler each morning of the tourney and tool on out to the Gulf Stream. At Stuart, at least two days of dress rehearsals and reconnaissance are *de rigueur*.

The first step is to assemble the right cast of warriors. For a group of anglers (who want to fish the tourney's team category) or a solo angler (who wants to compete in the pro or amateur divisions), this means finding the right boat (one that has a large cockpit, decent speed to get out and back fast, and enough stability to stand up to the Atlantic's swells), a first-class captain (one who knows how to go after sailfish) and a first-class mate (who knows how to prepare the baits, feed out the lines at the proper distances, and keep the entire cockpit operation running smoothly).

Once you've got the personnel and equipment and have arrived at Stuart, it's time to do your homework. Local tourney anglers usually know the area waters fairly well, but out-of-towners have to pore over the charts—checking water depths and looking for drop-offs where baitfish (and thus sailfish) tend to school. The next step is reconnoitering, going out to the fishing grounds, checking drop-offs with your straight-line recorder, and looking for weedlines which attract baitfish and often denote drop-offs.

Finally, it's time for rehearsals under battle conditions. The captain experiments with trolling speeds (usually around 700 r.p.m., depending on whether he's headed up sea or down sea) and baits (balao, mullet, or strips of bonito). The mate works on coordinating the four lines that have hooks and bait (two from the clothespin rigs on the transom, two from the out-riggers) and the hookless teasers (often plastic skirted lures) that are trailed off the transom to help raise the sailfish. A solo angler works on his reflexes and technique. A team of anglers plans who will fish when.

By the afternoon before the tourney's first day, the boat, gear, and personnel are ready to go. Or, as Bernard Muckenfuss says, "Nothing can happen that we aren't prepared for in one way or another."

On the night immediately preceding most battles, it's customary for all the troops to gather around the campfire and write letters home while a harmonica player bleats out a plaintive tune, preferably "Greensleeves" or "When Johnny Comes Marching Home." The Stuart version of this rite of war is a cocktail party *cum* fish stories, where the participants sip scotch and trade tall tales and generally hobnob. Blue blazers and white jackets (splattered with fishing tournament patches) are in abundance.

For many anglers, half the attraction of tournaments is the social life of dinners, cocktails, and award banquets. These are the rare occasions when dozens of outstanding anglers with like interests can talk shop and discuss technique.

Neophytes can hear such pearls of wisdom as, "The ideal situation is to catch a smart sailfish and a stupid one at the same time. The smart one takes off with the bait and the dumb one swims up to the boat so you can get him out of the way quickly. Then you can go to work on the smart one knowing you've scored already. Get one out of every three smart sailfish in the boat and you're doing fine."

After the party is the obligatory pre-tourney briefing, where the rules of sportfishing's Geneva Convention are reviewed: 20-pound-test only; single hook; no live bait; tag and release any fish you don't want to keep for mounting; a catch is consummated when the wire-leader's swivel touches the rod tip; the boat must be dead in the water as soon as a strike hits; an official observer must be on board each boat; the angler must set the hook and reel in the fish by himself. And so on. Then off to bed.

As angler Robert J. Miller is discovering on this, the opening morning of the tournament, sailfishing is 99 percent sitting. Promptly at 9 a.m. the lines were tossed overboard as Miller's *Lady Margaret*, a 46-foot Bertram Convertible, probed the Gulf Stream across Six-Mile Reef. Now, three-and-a-half hours later, all Miller has to show for his efforts are a sore butt and a couple of nibbles. The tourney so far seems like the opening rounds of a prize fight, the two adversaries testing one another without coming to any serious blows.

Once or twice a sailfish's fin has been spotted cutting through the water just beyond the baits as they dance across the waves, yet the sailfish refuse to move in and take a bite.

Miller, a mild-mannered guy in his late sixties, can do nothing but wait patiently in the huge Pompanette fighting chair. This is his third Stuart tournament, and he knows all too well that they also fish who only sit and wait. Last year he caught only one fish on opening day and went on to take third place in the tournament's professional division. This year, he's a pre-tourney favorite. He certainly holds enough trump cards. His Bertram is in top fishing form—twin turbo-charged 871-T1 diesels, 36-foot Rybovich outriggers, Penn reels, a homemade rocket launcher, and a Ross chart recorder.

The captain of *Lady Margaret*, Carlton Williams, has been tournament fishing for a decade and is regarded by his fellow captains as one of the best. The mate, Bob Ibsen, has teamed with Carl for eight years. Together they have refined tournament fishing to a science. Constantly checking water color, depth, temperature, and wind direction, they instinctively know where to fish and which baits to troll when.

Though this morning hasn't been one of their better outings, the overall effect aboard *Lady Margaret* amounts to the kind of coordination that is the hallmark of a highly skilled team of surgeons. Everything is done so efficiently and so silently that one forgets he is watching a sportfishing expedition. Judging by the lack of levity and conversation, one would think he were watching a heart transplant.

Up on the bridge, Williams guides the 46-footer slowly across the reef, keeping the techs glued to 700 r.p.m., working the weedlines and monitoring the chart recorder as though it were an EKG. Ibsen tends to the lines with dispatch, and Miller mostly waits, puffing on his pipe and cupping his hands. The only sound is the crackle of reports from other fishermen over the radio.

Even when the trio gets their first strike at 12:45 p.m., the detached efficiency continues. No panic, no barking of orders, no wasted motion.

Williams shifts the engines into neutral. Miller picks up the reel and inserts it in his leather fighting belt. He pauses until he senses the sailfish has taken the bait and then, with a precise flip of the rod, sets the hook. The battle is joined. Ibsen swiftly reels in the other lines to prevent any tangles that might allow the sailfish to escape. Williams keeps the transom perpendicular to the fish. Miller reels in with steady motion.

It is a dumb sailfish. He swims up to the boat and, a moment after the swivel touches the rod tip, manages to break free and disappear into the deep. In the space of four minutes—unusually swift for landing a sail—Miller and Co. are on the scoreboard. The three surgeons exchange smiles briefly and go back about their business.

At day's end, their six-and-a-half hours of fishing have produced just one catch and a couple of near-misses. Except for one boat with two fish, no one has fared much better. Only twenty-three fish have been caught the first day.

The casual approach to tourney fishing is quite evident aboard *Vin Van*, a 45-foot Hatteras, on Day Two. The boat's owner and angler of some note, Vincent Ross, Jr., has been detained in Palm Beach on business and has sent his stepson Mark Healy in his stead. Mark has never caught a sailfish in his life, let alone the first day of the competition, so today he intends to relax, enjoy himself, and perhaps even catch some fish.

Young Healy's inexperience notwithstanding, *Vin Van* and crew are another superb fishing team. Captain Ed Eaton spent his boyhood crewing on charter fishing boats along the Jersey shore and, after a stint as a top salesman for the 3M Corporation, has shucked his briefcase and necktie for the life of a tournament fishing captain aboard *Vin Van*. Ross and he have finished near the top in four of the eight sportfishing events they've entered. Mate Ronnie Cavanaugh, in his early twenties, has seen enough tourney action to handle the cockpit duties with skill.

Vin Van is six years old. Aside from the color TV and the eight-track stereo, she is a floating tackle box—cabinets full of reels, drawers stuffed to the gills with teasers, wire leader, hooks, lead sinkers, and similar ilk. Rybovich outriggers. Gin pole. 871-GM diesels. A fighting chair that would do any barber shop right proud.

The sails could care less. Like yesterday, the billfishing on this cloudy Friday morning has started off slowly. Healy is logging some practice in the meantime, first catching a dolphin at 9:30, then a football-sized tuna at 10:15. Eaton, who has taken up residence on the flying bridge, sits sideways in the helm chair, rocking back and forth.

His right eye monitors the lines, his left the Konel chart recorder, the tachs, and the sea ahead. He leaves his station only to get another pair of beers, which he systematically polishes off in between singing Mitch Miller tunes and shouting at the fish (wherever they may be) to get hungry. Not quite as formal or as silent as the Williams approach.

Eaton's battle strategy differs from Williams' as well. Instead of keying on the weedlines, Eaton is headed fifteen miles north to one of his favorite fishing spots before the day's fishing has gotten under way, and he now works down sea at 650 r.p.m. in depths around 120 feet about eight miles offshore. Captain Ed, who asserts that one of the tricks to sailfishing is knowing your boat, says that his Hatteras is one of the best "raising" boats—she has a knack for attracting sailfish up from the depths—especially running down sea.

In the cockpit, Healy is sitting in the fighting chair and swinging his legs in rhythm with the rock music that's piped in via a pair of speakers mounted above the salon door. He is wearing a T-shirt, flared jeans, and a painstakingly faded denim jacket—not standard fishing togs, but then he doesn't profess to be a fisherman. He almost takes comfort in the fact that not much is expected of him, being a rookie and all.

Such a relaxed approach (any more relaxed and it would be a party) would not seem conducive to sailfishing, but darned if Eaton doesn't begin to raise sailfish and double-darned if Healy doesn't catch one. After several far-misses, at 12:15 a school of sails hits several of the baits at once. A bit of chaos follows as Healy does a game of musical rods, picking one up, trying to set the hook unsuccessfully, dropping it and grabbing the next and then the next until he sets a hook good and solid. Cavanaugh scurries off to reel in the other lines while Eaton shouts instructions from the bridge.

Healy hangs in, pumps, and reels. At the other end of the line there is a decided lack of resistance. Three minutes later, a young sailfish, no more than twenty pounds, is boated. Healy beams. The rookie has just gotten his first hit in the majors. He sings along to the next song and quaffs his can of Busch, as if to say that maybe this tournament fishing stuff isn't so bad after all.

His enthusiasm is firmly entrenched when *Vin Van* hits another school at 1:30 and the Chinese fire drill begins anew. There's action on all four lines, and Healy once again sets a hook on his third try. Cavanaugh clears the other lines and stands behind the fighting chair to offer encouragement as Healy grimaces and reels for all he's worth. Ten minutes later, the swivel finally reaches the rod tip. Cavanaugh grabs the leader and tags the fish. It's over in a split second. Healy never gets more than a glimpse of the sailfish that has suddenly lifted him into the thick of the competition.

This second catch climaxes the afternoon. There's action on the lines after that, but Mark Healy can never quite implant the hook again, most likely because the sailfish's drop-back tactics have outfoxed him. On the day, he's had approximately a dozen solid shots at catching sails. He's converted only two, but it's good enough to put him in a four-way tie for second place in the professional division at the midway point of the tourney. Fishing has been so slow in the pro division that the four first-place anglers have a two-day total of three fish each. Among the leaders is one Robert Miller aboard *Lady Margaret*.

Day Three, which turns out to be the last day of the competition (Day Four is cancelled because of heavy seas), is marked by 6-foot swells and a shipload of caught sails—57 in all. Mark Healy is shut out, but Miller and *Lady Margaret* come up with four more sailfish to win the professional division. The three-day totals are nothing to write home about. Sixty-three fisherman have caught 137 fish, an average of .72 fish per day per angler.

With the anglers stuck in port because of the rough waters, it's not surprising that Sunday is rather moribund around the Bay Harbor Club. The top tourney anglers have met the sailfish on the high seas for three days, and overall you'd have to say the sails came out the winners. All the fishermen can do is wait for the Atlantic to calm down. Only then can they head for home and begin to plot their revenge.

5

Light Displacement

Stopping Freighters

by Rodney Strulo

APRIL, 1964

Freighters are like women: The best way to make a hit is to pretend you haven't noticed them.

Most yachts crossing from the Canaries to the West Indies don't reckon to meet any merchant ships, although single-handers sometimes worry about it. Frank, on the *Elsie* from Miami, plotted all the shipping lanes on his Pilot Chart and said he was going to stay awake when he crossed them. My wife and I often wonder what happened to Frank because when we sailed across in our cutter *Frisk* last year, we saw twelve ships—none of them on Frank's shipping lanes. But then we were probably longer on the voyage than he was. We took thirty-five days in fact, most of it spent becalmed.

We had been five days at Lat 16.24N Long 31.40W when we saw the *Soya Atlantic*. I had taught Heather to play chess; she had taught me how to wash up; we had read everything on board. That evening I had found a previously overlooked scrap of newspaper wrapped around a salami sausage and was going through the classified ads in my bunk. Heather was in the cockpit peeling potatoes. When I heard her let out a strangled gasp, I ran out on deck. She pointed the peeler at a big white freighter sailing across our bow. It was the first vessel we had seen, and we got very excited. We stood waving until she disappeared. Then we exhaustedly discussed her route, speed, course, destination, and cargo. But to our surprise, the *Soya Atlantic*, Stockholm, came back over the horizon shortly after and stopped close by.

"That was a quick trip," Heather murmured. We motored over in the dusk. Her hull loomed up enormous.

The captain shouted down through a megaphone:

"Do you need help?"

"No thanks. Bon voyage."

"For why were you waving?"

"Just being friendly," I said tentatively.

"When a merchant ship see a sailing boat signal, she think she is in distress."

"But when we saw you stop, we thought *you* were in distress." Some laughter from his crew, which didn't seem to help. He shone a searchlight on us.

"Where are you from?'

"Ibiza."

"Where?"

"Southampton, port of registry."

"London!" At this a lone voice on the freighter let out a cheer. Then we heard a splash in the water, and a cry of "Man overboard." Searchlights and commotion on the ship's deck high above us. We saw a man's head in the water.

"Throw him the life belt!" I said.

"But it's our only one. It'll ruin it, and anyway he doesn't need it. He's swimming over."

And indeed he was. He dog-paddled alongside then clambered over the rail—dripping, grinning, and huge. He seized my hand in a giant's grip:

"Hallo mates! I'm coming with you."

"You're what!"

"Yes, I'm from London, too. Stepney. I can't stand those Swedish bastards. You see, the police put me on board of her after I jumped ship in Brazil. They've been giving me a bad time, and I've 'ad it.''

Heather and I looked at one another.

"But we can't take you. We don't have enough food and water for one thing.''

"Aaaah! Don't worry about that. Ere!'' He whistled up at the heads lining the ship's side: "Give me my passbook and give me some food.''

"We don't want him,'' shouted the men above. "You keep him.''

"We can't possibly take him.''

"Give me my passbook; give me some food.''

An officer leaned out shaking his fist:

"You wait till I get you on board. I'll give you your passbook.''

The captain, completely lost, bawled through the megaphone:

"How many merchant seamen have you aboard? Who is your captain?''

We ignored both these questions, and everyone fell silent. Deadlock. We could hear the waves slapping against the side of the ship. A generator hummed.

"OK mates. I'm going back,'' said our sailor quietly. He looked smaller. He shook hands with us ceremoniously. "Best of luck. You've got some guts, you know.'' I didn't feel we had at that moment. He jumped in and swam to the freighter. They lowered a ladder for him. Their screw turned, and in a few minutes they were gone.

We were ghosting along in Lat 15:30N Long 59W when another big ship passed close by. For days we had drifted through schools of jelly fish and sea cucumbers, Portuguese men-of-war, and creatures like a little coral umbrella with feet sticking out from under it. December 8th was our big day—we overhauled an electric light bulb.

On the 9th we saw a freighter coming up rapidly astern.

"Oh no, not again,'' said Heather, and we went to hide in the cabin. Through the porthole we read *M.V. Enrico Dandolo, Venezia*. Then we heard them calling and came out.

An officer was on the bridge with a megaphone:

"You want anything?''

Well, we don't have a radio and are always glad of a chronometer check.

"What time is it?'' I pointed to my wrist; the officer waved and went into the wheelhouse. He came out again just as they drew out of range:

"Half-past three.''

A half-mile ahead the *Enrico Dandolo* stopped. We were still muttering "Half-past three," when we came up to her twenty minutes later. Heads crowded her rail, someone called "Catch!" and lowered a basket. I steered as close as I dared.

From the basket we tipped out loaves of crusty bread, three cheeses, cigarettes, that week's magazines, two flasks of Chianti, and, pinned to one of the flasks, a piece of paper with our position and course and distance for Barbados.

For Lack of
a Flag

by Peter Hird

OCTOBER, 1968

"So we'll be taking no red ensign with us when we sail, no old red duster then?"

"No, Jim," I answered, "we shall not. There's going to be no flag-waving of any sort. I'm not much on flags. It's too difficult to know what you should fly on what occasions. Fly the wrong one in the wrong place and everyone's offended, and anyway we're only sailing across the English Channel as far as Calais and Gravelines; we're not emulating Chichester, you know."

"Still," said Jim, "I think we ought to have the ensign. Give us an air of distinction and tell the French we're English."

"Look, Jim, the French will know you and I are English and guess you're Cockney, too, without our waving any ensigns at them; and we should hardly look distinguished sailing a small sloop with a red ensign almost bigger than the mainsail. The boat's too small. We can't fly one; there isn't room. Also, I haven't got one, and I don't intend to buy one. Ensigns cost money, and there isn't all that much cash to spare.''

We did, however, have one small, plain yellow piece of drapery for hoisting when we first got into France—to tell the French customs we'd arrived, but we didn't have to buy that specially. It was the yellow duster we used for cleaning portholes and rubbing up the compass.

From Dover we sailed without too much difficulty across to Calais and then to Gravelines. Those who've visited this small French harbor will know that the little port is a bit north of Calais—between Calais and Dunkerque—and that, like Calais, it has its two projecting arms but, unlike Calais and more like Margate, when the tide runs out there's very little water left. The French have, however, constructed an inner harbor entered through lock-gates, and here there is always water, for the gates are opened only at high tide. Seen from up above, Gravelines must look rather like a front door key; the rounded end is the inner harbor and the shank is the tidal channel up to it where the fishing vessels chiefly lie.

It was to one of these fishing vessels that, on entering Gravelines after a spot of trouble on the harbor bar, that we first tied up and then went to have a meal of steak and seaweed washed down with local wine. When we got back, the tide had ebbed completely and there was virtually no water left; still, the fishing vessel to which we were tied kept us in balance and roughly upright. The following morning and sometimes before high water, however, they announced that they were going out.

''If you wish water to float in,'' said the fishermen, ''then motor to the inner harbor on the tide, signal to them that you want to enter, and they will open for you.''

We started up the engine and with the tide at flow behind us made for the inner harbor. The fishermen were right; there was a man standing ready to work the gates and let us in. We courteously waved to him and also shouted. He waved back and shouted, too, but with the banging and thumping of the engine I couldn't catch his words. I took them to be greetings framed in French. But he did not open; we were excluded. We turned to sheer off the gates and circled and shouted once again; it was strangely similar to attempts at getting into the Common Market and attended with about the same success. The second lot of shouting had no more effect than did the first except that this time the gateman not only shouted but jumped up and down and waved his arms as well.

I asked Jim to run forward, not because he speaks good French but because he shouts loudly. Jim really has no French at all but he does know *Ouvrez la porte*. I forgot, however, in the small excitement of arm-waving that Jim's tenuous hold on French would not allow him to comprehend and pass on any message vouchsafed him by the keeper of the gates. The lock-gates, even though Jim said his piece in French and the situation seemed pretty obvious, still did not open, and again we turned.

"What did he say, Jim? He was shouting something."

"I don't rightly know, Pete. A bit like *'la la yure yure donk'* with every now and then a word like *'po'* and then he kept pointing to the mast, but there's no trouble there. I don't know what he's on about but if you ask me, he began to get annoyed and isn't going to let us in."

While I was turning this over in my mind and circling once more and wondering why the man should have been annoyed and wished to keep us out, Jim shouted: "Hoi, watch out astern. Seagoing vessel, large and cracking up at quite a lick. We're in her path."

And just at that moment the gates began to open. To have tried to rush them, to trundle in ahead, would have been to court disaster, collision with the entering ship or at the very least a good deal of bad temper; so we took the alternative action and as the vessel slowed to pass between the gates we shot in close behind her. The gateman tried to shut the gates and keep us out, and he very nearly did. But not quite, for gates against water come to rather slowly, and while they were still half-open we squeezed between them with just a rubbing of the strakes.

The French did not, I think, like this. I had the feeling that they felt, and probably correctly, that they had been defied.

We had hardly time to tie up in a corner of that pleasant and peaceful little harbor, something like an outside pond, before the gendarme came.

He was not full of *bonhomie* and *joi-de-vivre* or at all like the gendarme in those advertisements where he takes the tourists' guidebooks, holds up the Paris traffic for them, and welcomes them to France. He did not offer his salutation *les plus distinguèes* but came bluntly to the point.

"Messieurs," he said, addressing me and Jim, "what nationality are you?"

"English," I answered.

"You have your passports and your papers?"

I told him that we had and then produced them.

"They appear to be perfectly in order. Why then did you not fly your English flag when you came in? You enter illegally. The gatekeeper tried to keep you out until you showed your flag, but he was not successful, for you sneaked in behind the *Belle Etoile*. It would have been your misfortune, Messieurs, had he hit you with the lock-gates and sunk you; and I can assure you that had he done so the responsibility would have been entirely yours."

As my French is not good enough to allow me to talk at any length or at all convincingly on the psychology of flags and why I do not, myself, much care to fly them, I answered simply: "We do not have one."

"But you must have one, Monsieur, and your determination not to wave it is offensive to myself and France. You must have one for, otherwise, how do you get out of here?"

"Oh, much the same way that we came in, I fancy, under engine."

"No, Monsieur, I do not mean in what fashion are you going out. Your French is not so bad you cannot understand me. I mean how do you intend to accomplish it without the hoisting of your English flag—the *drapeau anglais*? I shall not let you out and neither will the gatekeeper, not until you hoist it on your boat to tell us who you are."

"But this is silly. You know who we are, you have seen our passports and the Dover Emigration Office papers."

"Monsieur, it is not silly, *ce n'est pas bête*, it is the maritime law of nations and one to which your country being, as it is, an island, strongly adheres. Any vessel entering a foreign harbor will show her national flag and she will do the same on leaving and all the time she's there. And I would add, Monsieur, that it would be a courtesy were you to display the flag of France as well."

And then he left us. This not waving of the English flag, contrary to what I had expected, had made a very bad impression. It is difficult to know quite where you are with flags. Wave the wrong one in the wrong place and they'll arrest you, as Americans and English know full well to their cost; but at other times, if you wave none at all, the situation is about the same.

"What are you going to do," asked Jim, "send home for one? I think he's going to make it a bit sticky when we have a shot at getting out."

"Of course not," I answered. "We can't sit here for days and days in deteriorating weather while a letter gets to England and they sort the drapery out and send a parcel back. And anyway there may well be something in the French customs regulations that utterly forbids importing English flags to France. It's surprising just how touchy nations can be with flags. Sometimes they look upon them as subversive and as an incitement to revolution. We had better, once again, rely on luck.''

But we could not sneak out behind any outgoing vessel for there was only the *Belle Etoile* in the inner harbor, and she showed no sign of moving. We had to approach the gates solo at high water. The keeper of the gates was there. He didn't open. We went round and round shouting, *"Ouvrez la porte"* and as an afterthought, to be polite, we this time added *"s'il vous plaît."* But it did not please him, he wasn't listening, and he refused to push the lock-gates open.

"He wants that flag, that's clear," I said to Jim. "Try him with the yellow duster."

Jim waves the yellow customs duster, but they're not fools in Gravelines. They can tell their hawks from hacksaws and red from yellow; so that didn't work. And they'd got us. They are a cunning lot in that little harbor. They don't open the gates naïvely at high water and leave them open until the tide begins to turn. The gates are shut, and they remain so until you can produce your tribal drapery and get them opened. And at high water there is not much time before the tide begins to turn. You can't afford to play about.

My friend Jim's knowledge of French is rather less than mine, but his knowledge of the world and its ways and of a variety of little dodges, is infinitely greater. If you're brought up in East London in the shadow of Bow bells, I guess you learn them.

"You okay alone on helm and engine, Pete? Right then, now cruise up gently towards that josser on the quayside, the gateman, and I'll use the boatpole on him."

"God! Jim. Strike him with that, even in righteous anger, and you'll have us both in the clink."

"Just you swing us near him," said Jim, "so that I can reach him. I'm not going to clonk him. I'm going to use a paper flag, a small communication, but as it's small we shall have to be near enough for him to see and recognize it and get the message."

Well, the paper symbol *was* small, stuck on the sharp point of the boatpole, and there was no red ensign printed on it, but the gateman's eyes were good and he recognized it, and Jim was right. The gates swung open and we sailed.

I should not, myself, have much cared to try the same maneuver on the gendarme, for had it failed the retribution would have been appalling. How long they give you for attempted bribery of the French police I'm far from clear, but probably a darn sight longer than for failure to be exuberant and wave your party flag.

Yet the whole thing did teach us a lesson: that in some places five-franc notes are as good as ensigns, indeed far better for you don't have to haul them up and down dramatically with halliards, and the effects that they produce seem pretty much the same.

The Fine Art of
Meta-Navigation

by James Lipscomb

APRIL, 1976

Most navigational systems have fancy names. There is celestial navigation, great circle navigation, navigation by dead reckoning, etc. To that
well-known list I would like to submit two additions: *touch-and-go*
navigation, which is akin to parking a car by sound, and *inferential*
navigation, which utilizes aesthetics and psychology.

Each year thousands of craft migrate like birds from the northeast
to Florida and return in the spring. Many of these voyagers are well-
equipped with Loran or radar or with well-educated navigators who can
pinpoint their position with a sun sight. This article is not for those
happy warriors. They know where they are most of the time—at least till
the generator breaks down, someone drops the sextant, or the radio fails.

This article is for small-boat operators like myself, who brave the ocean seas without expensive navigational aids and without any reasonable hope of determining their position by taking sun sights. For us, navigation is more than a science. It is a meta-science—an art.

My meta-navigational skill grew considerably two years ago. In the fall, I had just completed a couple of films of the America's Cup. Wanting to get away, I took my Tartan 30 to Florida.

It was on the Waterway during this trip that we learned touch-and-go navigation. The water on most sections of the Waterway is opaque. There is so much sediment in the water, I expected our depth sounder to register bottom at six inches. Actually, a Tartan 30 draws five feet, and there were many times on the trip when the depth gauge registered four-and-a-half. Whenever it did that, however, we had other ways of knowing that the water was shallow.

Really, any conscientious navigator ought to be able to keep off the mud on the Intracoastal. It's just that the mud is soft, the way is long, and the incentive is not quite so harsh as it would be if the bottom were coral. Red right, black left, black left, red right, the markers go by. After a while you become hypnotized, or maybe the helmsman—excuse me, helmsperson—feels the need for a little variety.

Touch-and-go navigation calls for an instantaneous reaction to the feel of the keel kissing mud. You put the tiller over and swerve back into the channel. How do you know which side of the channel you are hitting? You don't. But if you don't swerve, you'll surely ground. If you do swerve, you've at least got a 50-50 chance of aiming back into the channel.

Besides, your subconscious usually tells you the right direction to turn. Your subconscious has known for some time you were off but couldn't get through the cockpit chatter.

Touch-and-go also works just fine in selecting an anchorage at the side of the channel. You head off slowly till you ground. Then, with a gander at the stage of the tide, you back off a hundred feet or so and drop the hook.

The real navigational test, however, comes on the trip north when there are obvious advantages to sailing far offshore—provided the weather is not so inhibiting. First, the coast from Florida to Cape Hatteras is in the shape of a crescent. The direct line takes you offshore. Secondly, staying in the axis of the Gulf Stream can give you a boost of four knots in places, and the axis is well offshore except at both ends.

So you head for the axis of the Stream, the only problem being that once you are out of sight of land, you find yourself as devoid of landmarks as a tourist driving in Queens. Besides which, you are deep in the dread Bermuda Triangle.

When we sailed north last year, we had a succession of calms, headwinds, light air, and thunderstorms. It was nice sailing actually, just loping along or taking swims during calms. We had a sunshade over the cockpit a good part of the forenoon, and the afternoons were punctuated by some nicely violent thunderstorms.

Once we had whirling clouds overhead and a waterspout roiling the water nearby. We got the sails down just in time and caromed off at 5 knots under a bare pole. Hail the size of marbles added to the excitement.

After three days and two nights of this, I was not too sure where I was. For the benefit of the crew, I continued to place X marks on the chart to indicate our position, but mentally I kept drawing larger and larger circles as I made more and more guesses about the set of the Stream and tried to decipher the helmsperson's entries in the log. Under "course made good," one shipmate wrote, "Drifted a while, sailed 90° one hour, 30° for 20 minutes, 300° for one hour, and I don't remember what happened the rest of the time, but I had some nice thoughts."

Obviously, new techniques were needed, so I decided to fall back on inferential navigation. The First Law of this system is: If you don't know where you are, find someone who does and follow him.

Old sea dogs may feel that this form of navigation is beneath honoring with a name. It has been used, however, by no less a skipper than Ted Turner. In last year's Anclote Key race, none of the navigation equipment on Ted's new *Tenacious* was working. So he followed *Charisma* on the inference that they would know where they were. They did, and *Tenacious* saved her time and won the race.

As for us, we had ships all around us. Despite the number of wrecks one sees all over the world, we acted on the assumption that these fellows knew where they were.

Normally, the ships try to stay out of the Stream when they are going south, and stay in the axis going north. So as long as we kept the southbound ships inside to the west and the northbound ships tailgating us, we knew we must be near the axis of the Stream.

That didn't tell us, of course, how far north or south we were, but this trip holds one extraordinary boon for the inferential navigator. A westerly course will strike the continent somewhere.

Our need to apply this law arose sooner than we had expected. Our alternator threw up its hands and stopped working, and our lighting battery (one battery was saved for emergencies like starting the engine) was so low it wouldn't even run the running lights.

My calculations showed us to be off Jacksonville. This was confirmed by the late-night watch, who saw the loom of lights of a large city to the west. So I set a course for Fernandino, which is about twenty miles north of Jacksonville.

The light we picked up at dusk did not flash in the pattern described on the chart, and I was tempted to curse the Coast Guard for trying to confuse me. Then the binoculars revealed a great cement cross silhouetted against the sky. Now, there is only one huge cross on the coast of Florida and that is at St. Augustine.

It was immediately obvious to me, as it may be to some of *Rudder*'s more knowledgeable readers, that there had been some miscalculation in either my estimate of the Gulf Stream set, arithmetic, or day of the week.

I was not at first able to assign the error to any of these factors, but I did feel an obligation to maintain the morale of the crew, which calls for confidence in the skipper. I feared—rightly, I believe—that the revelation of a fifty-mile error in navigation might undermine their confidence, so in their best interest, I decided not to tell them about it.

Instead, I shaped a course northward from sea buoy to sea buoy to Jacksonville, where we arrived in the middle of the night. Not one to press my luck, I opted for standing off, in Hornblower tradition, until daylight. Then I boldly ran up the channel, which is a quarter of a mile wide.

Only one of the crew was in the least disturbed by the events of the evening, which I attribute to good showmanship on my part. However, one of the crew, Dr. Carl Cohen, a philosophy professor at the University of Michigan, has perhaps been corrupted by the scientific approach to these matters offered by Michigan's fine school of naval architecture.

Says Carl, "I thought we were at Fernandina last night."

"A fair assumption," says I.

"But we sailed north half the night and ended up in Jacksonville," says he.

"So it seems," says I.

"But Jacksonville is south of Fernandina," says he.

"That is an oddity," says I. "Perhaps this is Savannah."

My most successful use of inferential navigation occurred as we approached Morehead City, just south of Cape Hatteras. We had pinpointed our position at the outermost light off Frying Pan Shoal in North Carolina and then had headed for Morehead to take the Inland Waterway inside Hatteras to Norfolk.

We were out too far to see any navigational aids on the ninety-mile run, and my mental circles around our position grew steadily larger. The situation was further complicated because a thunderstorm was closing in on Morehead City the same time we were. Rain and mist surrounded us, and visibility was limited. Time for inferential navigation.

Fortunately there was quite a bit of evidence from which to infer. All over the horizon fishing boats of various sizes were just as interested as we in finding shelter. Since Morehead City is the only reasonably protected escape from the ocean in that area, it was relatively safe to infer that most of the boats were trying to make port. However, although most of the boats were headed more or less in a westerly direction, there seemed to be quite a disagreement as to the exact location of the channel.

Here the inferential navigator must fall back on his understanding of human nature as it is revealed in psychology and aesthetics. The Second Law of inferential navigation is: Never follow a boat with a cute name. For instance, never follow a boat named *Me Too*. The owner is probably as mixed up as you are. *Fat Chance* would also be a poor risk. A name like *First Mortgage* suggests a new boat owner who is still amazed at the cost of the thing. He probably hasn't finished his Power Squadron course.

Ah, but next came a nice fat Bertram with radar twirling on the mast, and you guessed it, the name was *Salty*. Only an old-timer with gimballed legs would dare use that name.

I never told the crew that I was following him, but the courses I set (after some hocus-pocus over my chart) accomplished that objective while maintaining my mystique. Sure enough, a half-hour later, the sea buoy off Morehead City appeared out of the rain, just where I'd said it would be—a triumph of meta-navigation.

The Making of
a Yachtsman

by Conrad Miller

MAY, 1963

I am a yachtsman.

I am not a boater, nor an inboarder, nor an outboarder, nor a sailing enthusiast, nor any kind of newfangled water sportsman. I'm a yachtsman.

Why do I claim the title yachtsman? Because I was raised in, on, and around boats. My father, brothers, and sisters all loved boats. We sailed under canvas, cruised under power, and generally gunkholed around Barnegat from my pre-kindergarten days. To my family, boats were always a way of life—not a way of making a living, but an avocation more serious than idle hobby.

Amateur boatmen loving the water are yachtsmen. I don't like to hear people called boaters, or outboarders, or sailboaters. The honorable word "yacht" has been altered by landsmen and status seekers to mean a large, private ship, very likely carrying a cargo of champagne and a crowd of rich stockbrokers complete with lady friends.

That, as Henry Mencken would say, is palpable buncombe.

A yacht is any boat used for sport, relaxation, or pleasure, and a yachtsman is one who operates a boat for fun and enjoyment. Only a pinched wouser or secluded reformer would claim it is sinful to operate a boat for pure enjoyment and relaxation. That's what boats, nay, yachts are for—enjoyment, health, fun.

What pushed the word "yachtsman" off into a corner with other half-bad words like "profit," "conservative" or "patriot?" Maybe they are old-fashioned words, but they are still good ones. Accurate, descriptive words have an honest place in the language even though given new, twisted meanings by journalists with leanings.

I am a yachtsman because when I was a school kid I used to sneak boating books and magazines behind the covers of the algebra text. I'd pretend to be studying, while drinking up boating lore and longing to be afloat. Boats, even the thought of them, were a release, an escape. Dreaming of water, beaches, and sails released me from the classroom and reality. My marks probably suffered, but my spirit did not.

Not that reality was unpleasant. I was raised in a home where boats were a common topic. Every winter morning I would go downstairs at 7:30 and grab *The New York Times*, not to read the news from Washington or other world capitols, but to glean news of frostbite sailing on Long Island Sound. Just reading about boats helped tide things over until spring when I could be afloat again.

How I counted the winter days waiting for the next issue of *Rudder*! William Albert Robinson was sailing *Svaap* around the world then and writing his adventures for *Rudder*. My dream was to follow in his footsteps.

During high school days (in the 1930s) my favorite books were Schoettle's classic *Sailing Craft*, and a salty, wonderfully mad book of the sea titled *Liverpool Jarge*.

Liverpool Jarge is a book you either read and throw aside in disgust, or read over and over again in delight. My younger brother, Fritz, and I read and reread *Liverpool Jarge* so many times the book became shredded. We used to quote whole salty passages and even complete pages of it to each other, laughing till we cried. Guests in the house would think we were crazy. But we were not crazy, just yachtsmen in the making.

As kids, we cruised our open, 16-foot sloop, *Vat-69*, on Barnegat Bay. The *Vat* was a stubby-masted, gaff-rigged sloop lacking freeboard, style, or speed. She was wet in the tiniest chop, but we kids loved our yacht and cruised it Huckleberry Finn style.

One night Fritz and I had been sailing off Waretown, where Barnegat's water is steep and choppy. It was late, and we were tired from a day of open cruising in the tiny sloop. The wind increased from the east; a dank drizzle started. To top our misery, the thermos jug broke, dumping the last of the hot coffee into the bilge. We were soaked, cold, unhappy. Fritz managed to light the kerosene lantern and rummaged in his duffle for something.

"What are you looking for?" I asked.

"The book," he replied. "I want to read a little of the gospel aloud."

"Good grief!" I shouted. "Things are wet and lousy, but we're not in danger. Belay the reading."

" 'Alagazoo, Zip Bang. You're asleep,' he says, 'You can't move.' "

" 'The hell I can't,' says Bull Taylor, very cross. And with that he fetches Jarge a cuff under the chops that knocks him clean across the deck, and he has to be carried below. That night, Jarge . . .' "

I burst out laughing. We both laughed, and he read until we had forgotten our soaked surroundings. Fritz was reading from our beloved *Liverpool Jarge*.

Since World War II there has been an emphasis on safe boating. Serious safety programs are needed because of new boat owners, many not raised on the water and lacking that inbred caution.

Safety programs remind me of things we did as youngsters. Perhaps they sound wild now, but I really think most were well-planned adventures. Anyway, they were part of a yachtsman's making.

In our 16-foot gaff-rigger, with sail and paddle alone, we used to challenge Manasquan inlet. This may shock some moderns who hesitate to tackle the nasty inlet with twin 300-horse engines.

Our secret, of course, was to play the tides. We would study and plot the tide flow. Then we'd ride the ebb tide out to the ocean in the morning and catch the flow back in the afternoon.

We stayed close to shore and always planned to beach the boat if a thunderstorm came up while we sailed the ocean waves. One August afternoon we had a chance to prove our strategy. A mean-looking black squall towered to the west of Bay Head. Getting back through the inlet was impossible. The tide was still ebbing fast, and sail power does not buck that kind of current.

We sailed close to the breakers, doused all sail, lashed things secure. Then with paddles we took the 16-footer through the surf and to the beach. A few feet from the sloping sand we dived and dragged the bow up the white beach. A dozen willing swimmers and sun bathers helped us pull the boat clear of the surf.

I remember sailing away after the squall passed. We pushed and paddled the boat out past the breakers, made sail, and headed north to the inlet. We were pleased with ourselves and proud of our boat handling. We were yachtsmen in the making.

Years later, on a less happy, darker day I was wading through the surf near Oran, North Africa. My thoughts flashed back to that pleasant landing operation at Bay Head. Thinking about it helped.

One summer at Mantoloking my brothers and I learned a lot about yachts and the gentlemen who build them.

The Mantoloking Boat Works was always referred to by us young scallywags as Scotland Yard, because our good friend, the chief boat-builder, was a Scotsman named Dave Beaton. Dave had a charming Scotch burr and a twinkle in his eye never to be forgotten. He loved boats and people. He particularly loved young yachtsmen in the making.

Dilapidated was the word for the old catboat, *Joy*, lying in the grass at Scotland Yard. The old yacht was so dry and the seams so open that grass grew in her bilge. She suffered from considerable rot, had broken frames and no rudder. But my brothers and I wanted her more than anything else. Dave said she'd been abandoned by her owner and if we'd pay the $25 yard bill she was ours, complete with a good sail. Pop staked us to the price and said he'd pay for paint, caulking, and materials.

Then we started.

For weeks we caulked, sanded, painted, fixed, and repaired. Slowly the *Joy* took shape. A yacht grew in place of the wreck.

Dave gave us lots of encouragement and expert guidance. One day he said, "Boys, you'll have to have a rudder made before you can sail the *Joy*."

"Right, Dave," we agreed. "Pop will make it for us. Cabinet work is Pop's hobby, and hardwood importing is his business, so he has the skill and material to build a good, big rudder."

So we asked Pop to make us a sound, substantial rudder for the catboat *Joy*.

And he made the rudder. Oh, dear Lord what a rudder! Never has such a rudder been seen before or since. To this day, *that* rudder is discussed by all who saw it. Especially it is discussed by the good Scot, Dave Beaton. The episode was almost thirty years ago, yet Dave always mentions "that rudder" when we meet today.

Pop is a cabinet maker by hobby. He imports hardwood by the thousands of tons as a business. What could be more natural then, that he pull a thick three-inch piece of beautiful, flame-grain mahogany from the rack and carve it into a rudder? That's just what he did. The rudder was one big lovely slab of the most flawless, thick mahogany I've ever seen. It was magnificent. It could have been a dining table in a baron's hall.

Dave took one look at that beautiful, golden wood, the flawless workmanship, the expensive flame grain. Then he looked at the miserable old *Joy*. It was too much for the good Scot.

"You can't do it! You can't do it!" cried Dave. "Mr. Miller, you just can't put a hundred dollar rudder on a twenty-five dollar boat!" Dave walked away shaking his head. "When you sell the *Joy*, please sell me the rudder," he pleaded.

We said we would.

But we never kept the promise. The *Joy* was lost in a northeast storm the following winter, and that beautiful mahogany rudder drifted somewhere down Barnegat Bay.

It was all in the making of a yachtsman.